FORGET
THE YELLOW
BRICK ROAD

LIZ GREEN

Successium Pty Ltd

Successium Pty Ltd
www.successium.com.au
www.lizgreen.com.au
Sydney, NSW, Australia

ISBN: 1-4392-4964-4
ISBN-13: 9781439249642

Visit www.booksurge.com to order more copies

Forget the Yellow Brick Road

Career development and training expert Liz Green has taken the story of Dorothy and her adventures in Oz to an entirely new and compelling place. In *Forget the Yellow Brick Road,* Green has crafted a story about success, determination, confidence, and risk-taking, all wrapped in the delightful parable of one girl's quest to reach her destination. While the original Dorothy is focused on getting home, the character in this career fairytale is headed in quite another direction: up the corporate ladder, preferably to the top. Teenage girls and women everywhere will celebrate Green's heroine as she learns to manoeuvre through the peaks and valleys of corporate life...with a few landmines along the way. In a voice that is both motivational and compassionate, the author uses her own corporate experiences to remind us that personal and professional success is found as much in the stops along the way as in the final destination. Those who grasp this concept and forge their own path will discover for themselves their very own Kansas.

To Mark,

my rock and support.
Your love and belief has made it all possible.

Contents

Preface

Let me take you on a journey, a career fairy tale. This is the story of Dorothy and her search for success.

CHAPTER 1

The Whirlwind

Dorothy lived in a spectacular home, perched high above the sea on an ocean cliff. She had designed this home with her husband of ten years, and it was their masterpiece, not just architecturally, but as a family home. It provided plenty of room for them and their two children and for entertaining family and friends.

Dorothy's favourite part of the house was the lounge, where, in winter, the suspended fireplace would flicker and toast her toes, and the moonlight would bounce off the ocean onto the cathedral ceilings high above her. She spent her favourite time of day, however, on the terrace overlooking the vast expanse of ocean in front of her, deep blue as far as she could see. As the sun faded at dusk, Dorothy often found herself reflecting on the day's events and all that she had achieved in her life and career.

Now a successful businesswoman, Dorothy had climbed the corporate ladder and shattered the glass ceiling. She enjoyed the thrill of corporate banter and politics and enjoyed working her magic in the boardroom. Her corner office provided expansive views of the city skyline, and her executive assistant was an invaluable resource who was at Dorothy's disposal any time of day or night.

In the years she had been working hard to get ahead, her daily ritual included walking from the train station to the office, along with the tens of thousands of other inner-city commuters. During these walks, Dorothy had gazed enviably in the passing windows of the designer clothes stores. She dreamt of the day when she would be able to walk proudly into one of those stores and purchase whatever her heart desired. That day came several years ago when Dorothy was promoted to CFO, chief financial officer. Of course there had been and were to be many more personal sacrifices she would make to meet the challenges of the new role, but buying that glorious suit without once considering the price on the tag was a small yet significant moment of success for her.

Dorothy's career had been everything she had hoped. Admittedly, she spent a few years studying at university before commencing her first role as a graduate accountant for a blue-chip organisation, but the climb up the ladder had been smooth sailing.

Her father had always told her that the way to the top was to complete your degree at university, commit to your career, and then pay your dues by working progressively up the ranks from graduate to analyst to manager to senior manager to executive general manager—just as he had.

Dorothy was pleased that she followed the career path her father had suggested. It was one thing to have achieved the position of finance director, but to then be awarded the role of CFO for a financial services firm was one of the highest recognitions she could imagine. Her father was so proud of her that she would often hear him boasting about her success to relatives during family events. Dorothy would quietly chuckle to herself when he would say that her success had a lot to do with the advice he had given her in the early years of her career: "Stick to the path, Dorothy, and it will lead you to where you want to be." She trusted her father and had followed the path, so to a certain degree she did have him to thank.

The privilege of being the company's CFO meant she travelled the world on business and was able to afford to take vacations with her family to some of the most secluded and exclusive locations. The family's most recent holiday was to a boutique luxury resort on a small island in the

South Pacific, where they were treated like royalty—a true escape to relax and unwind.

Dorothy had been sitting on the wicker daybed on the terrace for so long that the sun had completely disappeared and magical glittering stars appeared in the sky. On the distant horizon, over the ocean, a thunderstorm teased the night sky with a spectacular light show. There was no doubt, Dorothy's life and career were everything that she had hoped they would be.

"Dorothy, wake up, wake up! What on earth are you doing still in bed?" her father frantically yelled at her. "What sort of impression will you be making by being late on your first day at work? Get up, get ready. I suppose I'll have to drive you now. Hurry!"

Dorothy slowly transitioned from her dreamy slumber into a semiconscious state, until the words her father left bouncing around her room landed in her consciousness. "Crap!" she said. Dorothy stumbled out of bed and clambered to the shower, bewildered by how real the dream had felt. Thank goodness she had ironed her clothes last night, after spending hours attempting to decide on the perfect outfit for the first day of her first job. She had spent four years slogging it out at university and fought tooth and nail for this graduate position, so she needed the right clothes to reflect not just who she was today but who she wanted to be in the future.

In a twenty-minute whirlwind of activity, Dorothy had showered, wriggled into her clothes, blow-dried her hair, and done her makeup. She was ready. "Dad, what's holding you up? I'll wait for you in the car."

Dorothy swept up her bag and phone, checked her purse to make sure she had enough money to buy lunch, and grabbed a bottle of water from the fridge.

The drive into the city was quiet. Dorothy's father, Henry, was just as anxious as she was. This day was the culmination of everything they had planned. When Dorothy achieved the marks she needed to study accounting and finance at university, her father had committed to supporting her through her tertiary education. Now he saw it as his duty to make sure this all-important step of her first venture into employment was a smooth and successful transition that would lead to Dorothy's ideal career in accounting and finance—just as they had planned.

The voice of the GPS navigation system broke the silence: "Your destination is ahead in fifty metres." The traffic was moving incredibly slowly as the car edged forward a few more metres. Dorothy had at least five minutes before she would escape the silence of the car and step into the corporate world, a world unknown to her.

Henry took his hand off the steering wheel of the car and took Dorothy's hand in his. "Dorothy, just some final advice. Look at the path ahead of you. I want you to keep your eyes dead ahead, stay on the path, and not take your eyes off your end goal. Following that path with focus and dedication will be your best route to the top. That's how I did it, and I want the same for you."

Dorothy looked across to see her father's eyes well up with tears. "I know, Dad. I love you too," she said.

Seconds later, the traffic light turned green, and before Dorothy knew it, they had arrived outside the office building. They were in a no-stopping zone, so Dorothy quickly jumped out of the car and onto the pavement. Slamming the car door behind her, she waved good-bye to her dad, tugged awkwardly at her skirt, flicked back her hair, and looked toward the large glass revolving door of the building in front of her.

Forty-five minutes later...

CHAPTER 2

The Council with West

Dorothy was still sitting at the desk to which she had been directed when she first arrived. On the desk was a computer that she had turned on but had no idea how to log onto and a phone that looked more complex than the console of a spaceship. Despite the number of desks in the area, the loudest sound she heard was the whirl of the air-conditioning system. Occasionally a telephone would ring or the sound of a muted conversation would reach her from a distance. The atmosphere was sterile.

She was surrounded by grey partitioning with strategically placed glass panelling that allowed you to see if there was someone sitting in the workstation beside you. As Dorothy looked to her right through the partitioning, she saw a face looking back at her with much the same perplexed look.

Dorothy stuck her head around the corner. "It's my first day today."

"Me too," said the guy. "Are you in the graduate program too?"

"Yes, I am, and I have to admit I'm just a little bit nervous. I'm Dorothy."

"Sorry. I should have introduced myself. I'm Trent, and don't worry, I'm just as anxious. I definitely don't want to stuff it up!"

Trent stood up and shook Dorothy's hand with conviction. Dorothy had once read about the different kinds of handshakes and how they can be quite telling of someone's character—the knuckle cruncher, the dead fish, the superior, the double handed. The one Dorothy detested the most was the palm pincher. Some women only use a few fingers and thumb for the handshake, but it was infuriating when a man presented his hand and prevented you from firmly and properly shaking it, so you were left just grasping the tips of his fingers. To Trent's credit he shook her hand with a firm sense of equality and looked her straight in the eye. As a result Dorothy instinctively knew she was going to like Trent.

"Do you know how many of us are in the graduate program this year?" Dorothy asked Trent. During the summer break, Dorothy had been wondering what the final numbers would be as the economy had hit turbulent waters and there were news reports of redundancies being made in The Firm.

"I asked the same question this morning when I arrived," he said. "They said they have cut back graduate new recruits by fifty percent this year, so I guess we're two of the lucky ones."

Trent's eyes then shot over Dorothy's shoulder, and she noticed his expression change, so she discreetly swivelled her chair so she could look in the same direction.

Walking toward them was a group of the most serious-looking people she had ever seen. There were seven men and one woman. Like a mess of navy officers, they appeared to be marching, as if all stepping to the same internal beat. Dorothy and Trent slid back into their cubicles and faced their computers so as not to look conspicuous. Their flashing computer monitors' request to log in failed to help their efforts. The group of people sashayed past them without a sideways glance and slid into a meeting room.

Before Trent and Dorothy had a chance to speculate as to who the group of people may have been, Dorothy was tapped on the shoulder by their graduate recruiter, Nora. "Right, guys, it's time to head off to our orientation meeting. The others are already there and waiting," she said.

Dorothy and Trent obediently followed Nora toward the elevator past the meeting room into which the strange group of people had disappeared. "Do you know who those people are in that meeting room, Nora?" asked Dorothy.

"Well, actually, they are the senior managers that formed part of the graduate selection committee," responded Nora. She didn't notice Dorothy and Trent's shared glance of horror.

Without thinking, Trent said, "They don't appear to be the most friendly people."

Dorothy glared at Trent to signal him to be quiet. As they stepped into the lift, Nora defended the group of senior managers by explaining that they were selected for their exceptional accounting and financial expertise and for their contribution to The Firm.

"Actually, Dorothy, Sophia Williams is a senior manager and the only female senior manager part of the graduate selection committee," Nora said. "It seems she was rather impressed by your application essay and is keen to see you 'fulfill your goals.' Her words exactly. Here's hoping you fulfill her expectations!"

Dorothy could not help but notice Nora not so subtly roll her eyes as she looked down at her notes.

When they returned to their desks after the morning orientation meeting, Dorothy and Trent were pleased to learn these were to be their workstations for their first graduate rotation. They would also be working on the same team for the same manager. On their desks, each found a written memo on how to log into their computers and access their new e-mail accounts.

After opening her account, Dorothy noticed there was already an e-mail from Wendy West, their new manager.

> "Once you're back from your waste-of-
> time graduate orientation meeting, see
> me in my office at the end of the hall.
> WW"

Trent had logged on and was clearly reading the same e-mail because, when Dorothy looked through the glass partition at him, he was staring back at Dorothy with the same look of fear and trepidation she was feeling. Dorothy jumped up from her seat and headed toward what she could only guess was the "office at the end of the hall." She raised her hand to knock on the door, paused to allow Trent enough time to catch up to her, knocked, and then opened the door.

"Try again. I didn't say you could come in, did I?" barked Wendy.

Dorothy froze. It took her a few moments to comprehend what was happening. In front of her sat a perfectly groomed woman in her mid-twenties. She had glossy dark brown hair swept into a tight ponytail, flawless skin, bright red lipstick, and was dressed in a pinstriped navy suit. She yelled a second time. "I said try again!"

Dorothy backed out of the office, stumbling over Trent's toes behind her, and closed the door. They looked at each other, took a deep breath, and she knocked again.

"About time," said the voice from the other side of the door. "Hurry up and come in."

Dorothy opened the door with trepidation. She and Trent took seats opposite Wendy, who sat at her desk.

"There is no time to waste around here, and having those waste-of-time warm-and-fuzzy graduate meetings and training programs takes away from The Firm's ability to meet its objectives," Wendy said. "We can't bill your time off the job to the client, can we?"

Dorothy and Trent sat silently, stunned, and did not respond. They thought it was a rhetorical question, but it was not. "Can we?" Wendy said again, raising her voice.

"No," replied Dorothy and Trent in unison.

Wendy went on to lecture them about the necessity to meet budget and to charge each client as much as possible. Wendy also told them that she didn't have time to waste on training them, so they would have to sink or swim.

Wendy handed a large white binder full of paper and falling receipts to Trent. "Here, take this." she said to him. "I want you to reconcile all the expense forms and receipts by the end of today. And you, Dorothy, I will e-mail you a spreadsheet that someone was working on before they deserted me and The Firm for greener pastures. It does not balance, and I do not have time to work out why. You can do it. Now go. I have important work to do."

With that, Wendy swivelled her chair and returned to gaze intently into her computer screen. Without a word, Dorothy and Trent exited the office and shuffled back to their desks.

As promised, Wendy e-mailed Dorothy the spreadsheet. Dorothy opened it to find a galaxy of numbers with no meaning and no context. Hearing only the sound of the air-conditioning system, the faint sound of a telephone conversation in the distance, surrounded by grey walls, Dorothy's heart sank and she felt a tear run down her face.

Before Dorothy could wipe her tear away, Nora was at her desk.

"Have you met with your manager, Wendy West, yet?" asked Nora.

Dorothy could not bring herself to say 'yes', as if by not saying 'yes' she did not have to accept or acknowledge that the horrible person she just met was to be her manager. Trent was within ear shot sitting at his desk and could see through the glass portion of the partition that Dorothy was clearly upset and struggling to answer Nora. "Yes," he answered on their behalf.

Nora noticed that Dorothy was distressed.

"Look, guys, you have been selected for our graduate program because you are viewed as high-potential talent, and, trust me, we only hire the best and brightest," Nora told them. "You started with a goal, now keep your eye on that prize. We have a very structured career pathway here, and if you follow it, you can be guaranteed of success."

As swiftly as Nora had appeared, she disappeared, leaving Dorothy and Trent to fend for themselves as they embarked on their journey.

Three years later...

CHAPTER 3

How Dorothy Saved Scott

Dothy and Trent sat opposite each other, staring blankly into their drink glasses, at their regular table at the pub around the corner from The Firm. This pub had become a regular haunt for them since they began working together three years ago. From where Dorothy was sitting, she could see the pub quickly filling with the regular Friday night 'suits', in a kind of corroboree. On her left, she had a perfect view out the window. It was six o'clock in the evening, and just as a colony of ants march furiously toward their nests as rain approaches, so too were the office workers marching toward the pub as the weekend approached.

Dorothy and Trent had become the best of friends throughout their graduate rotations. Working for Wendy West had been the most difficult twelve months of Dorothy's life. It was only Trent's clever wit and support that had ensured she survived the ordeal. The two worked in separate departments of The Firm during their second rotation, which provided them both with an opportunity to expand their network.

Despite the fact that they were so different, they were an ideal team. Dorothy saw the big picture and was creative, optimistic, and heavily influenced by her external environment. Trent was focused on details, pragmatic, cynical, and internally driven. This balance worked perfectly for them while they were working on their final rotation together in the same department.

Their manager, Boyd McCarthy, was a good manager. Not only was he competent at his job, he also had a way with those who worked for him. He saw the best achieved by everyone on the team. People genuinely enjoyed working in his department. You could always hear chatter between colleagues or laughter after someone shared a joke.

Dorothy had always wondered why Boyd was not in a more senior role, especially considering how well liked he was by his team and the consistent results his department reported. In his mid-forties, slightly overweight, balding, and no taller than five foot five, Boyd was married with teenage kids. He had been the manager of the same department for almost nine years. The thought of working in the same job for nine years terrified Dorothy. Two years would be the most anyone should have to stay in the same job before being promoted, she thought–three years tops.

Dorothy remembered one afternoon when Boyd had called Dorothy and Trent into his office. It was a small office with a tiny window that faced a brick wall that seemed no more than an arm's length away.

"You have both done a wonderful job this last year," he said, "and it has been a pleasure to have you on the team. Your contributions have not been overlooked, it seems…." Boyd had paused, looking at Dorothy and Trent with eyes filled with pride.

Neither Dorothy nor Trent were the type to boast, so both had sat silently waiting for Boyd to go on. "Not only did you both successfully source your own permanent placements at the end of the graduate program, but you, Dorothy, straight into a business analyst role, and you, Trent, an auditor. Well done to you both."

"We are both really happy, Boyd, but you know we couldn't have done it without you," Dorothy said.

"Nonsense, you're good kids, and you would do well anywhere."

Dorothy had sensed that Boyd was a little disappointed that neither of them had chosen to stay with him and his team. It was not that they did not like Boyd and the rest of the team. It was just that they had all been there so long and seemed to be regularly overlooked for promotion, and neither Dorothy nor Trent wanted to find themselves in a similar situation. In fact, Trent had once commented to Dorothy that he thought that not one of them aspired to anything more than their cosy little cubicles, on their secure little floor, of the same building they had worked in for so many years. Dorothy could not believe that could be the case.

"Boyd, can I ask you something?" Dorothy asked tentatively.

"Of course, Dorothy, anything," Boyd said, without hesitation.

"You're such a great manager and fantastic at what you do, so why are you still in the same job as you were nine years ago?" she asked. "Surely you want to succeed?"

As Dorothy said the words, she regretted them passing her lips. She was surprised to see a look almost of pity on Boyd's face.

"Dorothy, the team spirit I have nurtured here is based on competence, hard work, respect, and a genuine liking for working together to achieve a common goal," he said. "We have a commitment to our jobs, but we also make sure we maintain a commitment to our lives outside of work. In other teams and departments, things are not always so supportive and conducive to those goals."

Dorothy responded defensively. "But surely it is worth the risk and challenge to be able to achieve success?" she asked.

Boyd stood up from his chair and paced slowly to the glass partition of his office to look out at his team. "Only if you want it enough, Dorothy, and only if that's what is right for you."

Now sitting at the pub with Trent, Dorothy, still staring into her drink, worried a little. She was almost certain that she was on the right path for her and bravely resolved not to turn back.

After Dorothy left Boyd's department, she found her new role as a business analyst to be intellectually stimulating, but she was again working on one of those grey floors with grey furniture and, in general, grey people. The saving grace, however, was that there were a handful of highly skilled and knowledgeable colleagues whom Dorothy found impressive. Consequently, she spent the first six months of her time in the role dedicating herself to learning everything there was to know and do.

In the second six months of the role, she was asked to form part of a cross-functional task force to work on a special project for human resources. Although human resources was not one of Dorothy's areas of expertise or interest, she accepted reluctantly with the hope it would look good on her résumé.

Ironically, this assignment turned out to be one of the most interesting projects she had worked on in her career to date. It had provided an opportunity to meet people from other departments and functions she may not have met otherwise. One particular individual left a lasting impression.

It was the fourth meeting of the task force. Given that all the participants had been communicating by telephone and e-mail between the meetings, and some had been working together on group tasks, they had got to know each other fairly well. At the end of the meeting, as everyone was rounding up their action task lists and heading out the door, Dorothy noticed Scott Crow sitting quietly in the corner with his shoulders slouched, appearing disillusioned. She slowed down the pace of her packing, waited for the room to empty of most of the participants, and then approached Scott.

"Everything OK, Scott?" asked Dorothy.

"Yeah, I suppose so," replied Scott.

Scott Crow was a team manager, so technically he was more senior than Dorothy and probably a few years older. He had been working in his role for a little more than two years. Today he looked a little more dishevelled than usual. His tie was loose, his sleeves rolled up, and part of his shirt was untucked and poking out the back of his chair. When Dorothy pulled out the chair next to him to sit, she also noticed one of his shoelaces was undone.

"You suppose so?" Dorothy said.

Scott looked up to see Dorothy earnestly looking at him, hoping to be able to help him, so he responded, "Why are we here?"

"That's a big question, Scott," exclaimed Dorothy.

"No, not the universal question, Dorothy! I mean why are we here in this project team? And I don't mean the obvious objectives of the project either."

Dorothy now knew it was not disillusionment she had seen. She was looking into the eyes of someone filled with self-doubt.

"Well, I can't say why you are here, Scott, but I know I am here because I want to be the best I can be and positively contribute to The Firm," she said. "And in doing that, I hope that will mean I will achieve all I set out to achieve."

"And what's that then? What do you want to achieve?" asked Scott.

Dorothy pondered momentarily and replied simply, "Success."

"I want that too, Dorothy. Well, I thought I did, but now I don't know. In fact, I'm not sure I know anything at all. I just had my performance review, and the feedback identified some performance gaps that I had no idea were an issue. I had actually been hoping for a pay rise and promotion. And then sitting here in this meeting today listening to you all, there was nothing I could contribute over and above what had already been said. Actually, some of the things that were suggested were so clever I was blown away. I just don't think I am smart enough."

Dorothy was surprised. She had always considered Scott as someone who was doing well in his career. His role on the project team had been as the fearless negotiator with senior management, and he seemed to solve problems and devise strategies to overcome barriers that had initially been considered as unmoveable by the team. In fact, she was envious of those characteristics.

She was perplexed and not sure how she should respond to Scott. It was rare for someone to express vulnerability around this office.

"Scott, I understand how you must be feeling," she said. "I know at times I have felt lost and doubted myself, but I have been lucky to have Trent and my father as sounding boards. Do you have anyone you can talk to about this kind of thing?"

Scott looked back at Dorothy blankly. It suddenly occurred to her that not everyone was as lucky as she was to have people who cared enough to listen or help. Without a second thought, she said, "You'll really like Trent. He's a good guy. We always go for a drink after work on a Friday night. You should come."

A few months later...

CHAPTER 4

Mountainous Terrain

Dorothy, Trent, and Scott Crow had become solid friends in the months since Dorothy first introduced Scott to Trent. As it turned out, they needed each other's support more than ever.

The economic crisis that was in its infancy when Dorothy and Trent had started as graduates with The Firm had now reached rock bottom, and the impact was felt around the world. Unemployment had reached an all-time high, and The Firm had not been spared.

Trent worked hard as an auditor, and he was good at it. In fact, he never got tired of sharing his success stories with Dorothy over their regular Friday night drinks. Trent's manager considered Trent a highly valued team member and selected him to be his eventual successor. Trent's uncanny ability to see problems coming and dodge them with agility was an admirable trait.

Three months before, to reduce costs, The Firm began to merge similar functions in different departments and close down teams in regional offices. Trent thought it made business sense for The Firm to merge his audit team with another. Although his team was fortunately operating out of the head office, he was concerned that his role and the roles of those he worked with might be threatened. Although Trent was not privy to any confidential information that would pertain to mergers or loss of jobs, he was certain something was cooking. Trent took his ideas and plans to Dorothy and Scott, and over many coffees, late into the evening in Scott's apartment, they would brainstorm and strategise.

Trent did his utmost to ensure his team was operating at optimum efficiency by convincing his manager to allow him to refine their standard operating procedures and implement a continuous improvement process. His strategy worked in his favour. When the two teams were merged and many lost their jobs, not only did Trent keep his job, he was promoted to audit team leader.

On the other hand, despite Scott's fabulous ability to solve problems and devise solutions, he tended to stumble his way along. Dorothy and Trent were amazed when time after time Scott would tell stories of his falls, but then in no time at all was back up on his feet again as though nothing had happened at all.

Dorothy was having the hardest time of the three. The downsizing, economising, and widespread fear of job loss intensified the environment as politics reared its ugly head. Some people headed for the bunkers to protect themselves, while others chose to step forward and fight. Dorothy watched as some soldiers won battles and others faced certain death on the battlefield. It became clear that Dorothy could not allow herself to cower in the bunkers or play dead and hope for the battle to pass her by. The need to rise to the challenge was no more evident than the day she learned that her department was to be closed down.

It was a deceptively beautiful winter's day—when the sun pours through the window and the sky is crystal blue, but the air is blisteringly cold once you step outside. After alighting from the train on her way to work, Dorothy dropped by the corner coffee cart to buy a large latte to sip on to keep her warm during the ritual walk to work.

On the lift ride up to her floor, everything was as it always was, with people staring straight ahead paying no attention to those around them. No 'hellos' or 'have a nice days'. For months after she first started working for The

Firm, it had bothered Dorothy that all those people in the elevator worked for the same company but did not make any effort to talk to each other. She had now accepted it as the way things were done, this morning the silence in the elevator was almost comforting.

Stepping out of the lift onto her grey floor, Dorothy's feeling of comfort was rapidly replaced with fear. In front of her, she saw too many people. At this time of the morning people were usually seated at their desks, hidden behind their partitions, beavering away. Today, however, they were standing huddled outside the floor's training room. As she approached the group, her phone rang.

"Dorothy, it's Trent," said the voice on the other end of the line.

"Trent, there's something strange...." whispered Dorothy.

"I know, quiet, just listen. Your department is about to be shut down," he said.

Dorothy's heart sank with a force that almost dropped her to her knees. This event was not in her plan. What was going to happen to her? How would she find a job in this market? Oh, the thought of having to walk into a job interview and admit she had been made redundant!

"Scott is off trying to find out more for you," Trent said.

Dorothy looked up to see that the hoard of people had been ushered into the training room. It looked like a scene from a World War II movie, when prisoners are being ushered into the gas chambers. A woman she did not recognise was waving her hand at Dorothy from the door of the training room, summoning her to join them.

"I've got to go, Trent. They're waiting for me," Dorothy said with a quiver in her voice.

"It'll be OK, Dorothy. It has to be," said Trent, with as much certainty as he could muster.

The announcement was horrific. The rumour was true. The department was being shut down, and redundancies were effective immediately. It was such a blur, and much of what was being said to them about business being business in tough times was like the stinging pain of saltwater on a fresh wound.

After the meeting, Dorothy could not get out of the room fast enough, as the imagery of the gas chamber consumed her thoughts. She could feel herself struggling for air.

Back at her desk, she began to slowly pack her belongings into her bag—a tube of hand cream that smelled like freshly picked roses, a bottle of multivitamins to assist her through even the toughest work weeks, and a framed photo of her with Trent and Scott at last year's office Christmas party. The last thing Dorothy took from her desk was a picture she had taped to her partition. It was of a mountain with its tip peeking through the clouds. The quote at the bottom read, 'Keep your destination in clear view'.

Dorothy was deep in thought when she heard a voice from behind her. "Are you Dorothy?" The voice belonged to the woman who had earlier waved Dorothy into the training room. "Could you come with me, please?"

The woman pivoted on the ball of her foot and strode back to the training room. Dorothy stood up to follow her and noticed that, although the floor was almost deserted, the few people who remained were well aware that this woman had just singled out Dorothy as they stared at her. Dorothy picked up her belongings and then put them down again, not sure whether she should take them with her or not. In the end, she decided to take them just in case, picked them all up again, and headed toward the 'gas chamber'.

Dorothy timidly poked her head in the doorway and saw the woman sitting with a man, waiting for her. "Please come in and sit down," the woman said. Dorothy sat down and clumsily dropped her belongings around her feet.

"Dorothy, I am sorry you had to receive the news you did today," the man said. "These are unfortunate times, and sometimes these things just have to happen."

Dorothy said nothing. She just nodded.

"Dorothy, we have been told, however, that The Firm has identified you as someone they would rather not lose," said the woman.

Dorothy looked down at her lap, took a deep breath, and waited for what she desperately hoped was coming next.

"So, we have been asked to offer you another position," the man said. "You would be responsible for formally closing down the operations of this department and merging its critical functions into another area of the business. You will be provided with a small team of people who have been identified as having a great deal of knowledge capital to support you."

"But what about everyone else?" asked Dorothy.

"Well, I would have to say that by the look on the faces of the people still outside this door, you will not be very popular," the woman said, chuckling and nudging the man beside her. "But hey, that doesn't matter, right. They will not be working here anymore."

An awkward silence fell among them. They were right, Dorothy thought. She was not going to be popular if she gained a promotion out of this. Even if the others were gone, they would still have friends in other departments who could make things difficult for her. But what's the alternative? Unemployment?

"Could you please give me a moment to make a phone call?" asked Dorothy.

The man and woman looked at each other in surprise. They both stood up and said they would wait outside the door for her. With trembling hands, Dorothy dialled Trent's extension. When he picked up the phone, Dorothy did not even wait for his 'hello'. "Trent, it's Dorothy. Can you conference-call Scott in?"

Within moments, the three of them were discussing Dorothy's morning and what had just been offered to her. Trent could not understand Dorothy's hesitation, but Scott did. At times like these, Dorothy appreciated Scott's ability to empathise.

"Dorothy," Scott said, "I know it seems tough and that things are going to get tougher. But if the road heads in, it stands to reason that it has got to come out at the other side then, doesn't it?" At that moment, the image of the mountain peak came into view.

Dorothy thanked her friends, hung up the phone, and walked to the door of the training room. "OK, I'll take on the role," said Dorothy said to the man and woman standing inside. They looked back at her with little concern. The man said, "Did we forget to mention that the role is only a temporary contract until the transition is complete?"

Exactly seven months later...

CHAPTER 5

The Rescue of Tim Woods

After Dorothy overcame the initial shock and worry of her new role being only a temporary one, she found herself engrossed in the task assigned to her. Managing a team of people, albeit a small one of three, was a role that Dorothy took to like a duck to water. Her compassion and openness ensured that her team quickly trusted and supported her. The project lasted seven months, which was longer than expected, due to the resistance of the remaining department to take on the additional responsibility and workload.

Coincidentally, Scott Crow was now the manager of the department into which Dorothy was responsible for transitioning the core functions of her previous department. It had been wonderful to have a friendly and supportive colleague to work with throughout the change-management process.

During this time, Trent had been busy building a reputation for himself in The Firm—and a reputation with the ladies. His boundless energy had ensured that he always had time to work hard and play hard, but also to always meet for Friday night drinks—a tradition Dorothy and Trent had started five and a half years before. The tradition now included Scott, who regularly joined them on Friday nights.

Now that Dorothy's project was finally coming to an end, two of her team members had found jobs in other firms and moved on. Just she and Tim Woods were left to tie up loose ends.

Based on her first impression, Dorothy thought the strikingly handsome, toned, six-foot-three Tim would be arrogant and self-absorbed. Instead, he was a genuinely nice guy.

Approximately four months into the transition project, Dorothy was working back late on some in-depth analysis and workflow documents that were urgently required for a training program. The documents had to be delivered the following day. Only on completion did she realise how late it really was when she was disturbed out of her trance by the sound of the cleaners vacuuming.

As she shut down her computer and gathered her things, she felt her stomach rumble. She was wondering what she would have for dinner considering it was so late in the evening. Heading toward the elevator she bumped into Tim walking out of the men's restroom.

"Haven't you gone home yet, Tim?" asked Dorothy. "I thought I was the only one silly enough to be here at this hour!" She rolled her eyes and shrugged her shoulders.

"It seems we are both gluttons for punishment!" replied Tim as he continued walking past Dorothy back to his desk.

Dorothy moved toward the elevators but then hesitated and called back to Tim. "Have you eaten yet? I'm probably going to drop into the Chinese place around the corner. Interested in some sweet and sour pork?"

Tim started to shake his head but then looked down at his own watch and realised the time. "Sure. Why not? Better than frozen pizza."

It was a beautiful evening. Spring brought with it beautiful warm days and fresh evenings with clear skies. Tonight was no exception. The sky attempted to peek through the office buildings towering high above them. Although the Chinese restaurant had only a handful of diners scattered at its tables, Dorothy preferred to order takeaway and eat their meals sitting by the harbour. After sitting inside all day in their grey surroundings, Dorothy insisted to Tim that it was necessary to their health and well-being to walk a little and breathe in some fresh air.

Perched on a park bench overlooking the harbour, Dorothy and Tim ferociously scooped their dinner into their mouths, as though it had been days since their last meal. As their food hit their bellies, they began to talk.

Dorothy shared with Tim the journey of her career to date—her experience in the graduate program after finishing university, her experiences with the dreaded Wendy West, her role as a business analyst, the excitement of working on the cross-functional task force, the shock of the department closing, and finally her selection as manager of the transition project.

Tim's story was a little different. Tim Woods was a handsome guy with dreams and hopes for his career that were well beyond what anyone else in his family had ever achieved. He remembered sitting at the family dinner table listening to his mother and father complain about their jobs each and every evening. When Tim was about fourteen years old, he asked his parents why they just did not go and get new jobs if they were unhappy and did not like the jobs they had. The solution seemed so obvious and quite simple to Tim. The question was not received well by Mr. and Mrs. Woods.

"When you're older, Tim, you'll understand," his father said. We are Woods, and Woods come from a long line of working-class people, proud of their place in life. It is not our place to question that or rock the boat. And even if we wanted to, changing jobs is too hard and too risky. We have a family to provide for, you know!"

At that moment, Tim vowed that he would never allow himself to be in the same position as his parents.

Tim stayed true to his word by working hard at school to earn a scholarship to study at university. He was the first Woods to graduate with tertiary qualifications. Finding his first job after graduating was not as easy as he had hoped, but within three months, Tim landed his first job, at The Firm.

Tim worked extremely hard and was quickly promoted to team leader due to his ability to cut through complicated issues and resolve them with little fuss and expense to the business. While in this role, Tim met Marianne, a sweet and charming girl in payroll. After a whirlwind romance, they fell desperately in love and eloped. In their first year of marriage, they became parents to a healthy baby girl. Tim loved being a family man and enjoyed the confidence his career gave him and the security it provided for his wife and daughter.

Three years ago, when his daughter was only six months old, Tim's wife was in a terrible accident and passed away. It was a gut-wrenching time for him. While having to stay strong for his daughter and continue to love her and care for her, he suffered with episodes of depression. He questioned the fairness of his beautiful wife's life being cut short.

"Despite my mother helping me out by minding my daughter while I'm at work, I just haven't been able to progress my career. The pressure of being a widowed single father has really hindered my success." Tim told Dorothy.

As Dorothy listened, she was saddened to learn that Tim's dreams and aspirations had been shattered. She had no idea that things had been so tough for him.

"So, have you started making plans for your next role? It will not be long until our temporary positions come to an end," asked Dorothy.

She wanted to ask him more about his wife and daughter but sensed he was close to tears and decided to keep the conversation work related.

"I haven't been offered anything, so I suppose they will let me go once the project is over," he said. His reply was tainted with fatalism.

With kindness, Dorothy replied, "Come on, Tim. What happened to those dreams and hopes you started your career with?"

As Tim looked out to the harbour where the boats enthusiastically bobbed and the city lights twinkled and sparkled with joy, he quietly said, "They're long gone now."

Dorothy decided all Tim needed was a plan. Actually, she would soon need a plan, too.

"You need to meet my friends Trent and Scott," she said "They have been great support to me over the years. In fact, you already know Scott Crow. He's the manager of the new department we are working with now. We go for Friday night drinks at the local pub every week." Dorothy was sure that Tim would get on famously with the boys, and meeting them was just what he needed.

Tim did not seem interested, however. In fact, he now looked even more disheartened. "Sorry, Dorothy, but I need to be home with my daughter. I like to read her a story and tuck her into bed at night."

Dorothy realised how inconsiderate she had been. If Tim was a single father of a three-and-a-half-year-old, he was not going to be able to go to the pub on a Friday night.

"Maybe we could find somewhere else to go?" Dorothy started.

Tim's eyes lit up. "I would be happy for you to come around to my place," he said.

The following week, Trent, Scott, and Dorothy met at Tim's house for Friday night drinks. Tim's house was warm and cosy, the floral curtains were the most obvious feature to suggest it had been decorated by a woman. The home was perfectly maintained. There was a family portrait of Tim, Marianne, and their newborn daughter proudly displayed on the mantel. Toys were spilling out of a toy box in the corner, and the distant sound of a musical lullaby drifted into the dining room from the end of the hall.

"I've brought pizzas," Trent exclaimed as he moved past Tim to place the boxes on the table.

"And I've brought the drinks," announced Scott.

While subtly keeping one eye on Tim, Dorothy said, "And I proclaim tonight we devise strategic plans to help me and Tim find our next jobs so that we know what we're going to do once the transition project is over."

Tim turned to walk into the kitchen, allowing himself a secret smile and a sigh of relief.

Another few months later...

CHAPTER 6

Catherine Lyons

Catherine Lyons had been working in corporate recruitment for several years now. Her plan was to use the role as a stepping stone into her preferred interest, which was to work in organisational learning and development. As it turned out, the career shift was not quite as simple as that. Catherine had found herself pigeonholed as a recruiter. She was fearful that, although she was good at her job, she would never be able to land her ideal job.

Raised in the country but with big-city dreams, Catherine was known for her warmth and honesty and a charm that enchanted those around her. After years of frustration in finding other people jobs and not being able to find one for herself, she began to take her frustrations out on those around her. She became brash and aggressive, traits she detested in others, let alone in herself.

Catherine was scheduled to meet with a potential recruit for a management position she was struggling to fill with the ideal candidate. She had spent weeks searching for and interviewing both internal and external candidates through referrals, but still no one met the brief. She doubted that the person she was to interview today would be any different from all the others, but because the woman was an internal candidate, Catherine was obliged to follow through.

After the transition, Tim had found a new job but was now no longer working for The Firm. With the help of his friends, he was able to identify what he really wanted out of his next job. Together they developed a plan that assisted him in successfully achieving the next step. Tim was now working closer to home and working shorter hours than he did when he worked for The Firm. He was also able to spend more time with his daughter, who was growing up quickly.

Dorothy, however, continued working for The Firm, as she was convinced that she was destined to stay on that path. She had hoped to find a more senior role because she loathed the thought of changing jobs without making an upward move. Management roles, however, were thin on the ground as The Firm had rationalised and reduced much of middle management to flatten out the organisational structure. When the transition project ended, Dorothy had to take a similar project role in another area of the business. Although the role was not another rung up the ladder, at least it was a sideways step, thought Dorothy.

After several months, however, Dorothy became bored and struggled to stay focused. In her head, she knew that if she let the quality of her work drop, others would begin to notice, and it could damage her chances for promotion. In her heart, she was losing motivation and knew she needed a new challenge.

Late one Friday night at Tim's house, as the four friends were chatting over coffee, Dorothy began to complain about not being happy in her job. This complaint was nothing new to the friends. They had been listening to the same story for weeks now. Trent was tired of being 'nice' and supportive and decided now was the time for them to snap Dorothy into action.

"Dorothy, what is it that you are waiting for? Someone to come and tap you on the shoulder and say, 'Hey, Dorothy, great job you're doing there, and I bet you're looking for another job. Why not come and work for me?'" Trent said sarcastically.

The group fell silent. Scott and Tim were reluctant to look up from their coffee cups, and Dorothy glared at

Trent. As the moments passed, still no one said a word. Scott could not stand the deafening silence any longer and broke the ice.

"He is right, you know, Dorothy," Scott said gently. "If you want that management job, you have to go out and find it. Waiting for the job vacancy to appear on the company intranet is not going to do it. You need to get out there, develop relationships, and get yourself on the radar of the people that matter."

Dorothy listened to Scott with resentment. She knew he was right. How had she found herself in this position? "You're right. You're both right," she said. "As of Monday, things will be different, and within three months, I guarantee you I will have that job!"

So, Dorothy set about networking with the right people. She also continued to work hard in her current role to demonstrate that she was capable and an ideal employee and manager. Within eight weeks, Dorothy was tipped off about a job. The Firm ideally wanted an internal candidate, but, to this point, it had not found the right person. She was given the name of the recruiter: Catherine Lyons.

On the morning of the scheduled interview with Catherine, Dorothy was nervous. It had been a long time since she had interviewed for a job that she wanted so much. Dorothy promised herself she would remain confident and self-assured; she would not appear desperate. Awkwardly sitting on a low and extremely soft leather armchair in the reception area, Dorothy struggled to sit in a fashion that looked comfortable yet professional. At times like these, she thought, why did it so often feel as though you were an animal waiting for slaughter? Dorothy did not have time to ponder the thought any further as Catherine appeared from behind the glass doors and invited her into the meeting room.

"So, Dorothy, what's so special about you?" asked Catherine abruptly.

Dorothy was taken aback by Catherine's direct question and dominating presence. Caught off guard, Dorothy began to stumble over her words, but she tried desperately to remain cool and calm under the pressure. The mood of the interview changed very little. Catherine aggressively barraged her with questions, while Dorothy attempted to respond with intelligence and grace. No matter what Dorothy said, it seemed that Catherine's opinion of her did not shift. She could feel the potential new job slipping through her fingers.

As the interview drew to a close, Dorothy felt the walls of the meeting room closing in on her. The wall clock to her right seemed to tick louder and louder with every second. Out of the corner of her eye, she could see the feet of employees passing by the frosted glass walls of the meeting room, seemingly at a running pace, as if to escape some horrible disaster. Little did they know, she thought, the disaster was unfolding in this room.

"Right. Well, that's it then, Dorothy," said Catherine. "Is there anything else you would like to add?"

There were so many things Dorothy wanted to say to make it all better, to fix this disaster, and land herself that management position, but the words escaped her. To her shock and horror, however, she did find some words. As Dorothy picked up her handbag and headed for the door, she said, "So, Catherine, what's so special about you?" Without waiting for her response, Dorothy left.

Dorothy's friends knew she had the interview that morning, so Trent and Scott arranged to meet with her for lunch for a debriefing. Dorothy was in no mood to go to lunch now, but she knew there was no escaping it and reluctantly made her way to the café.

When she arrived, she saw the boys sitting, eagerly waiting for her. They had been so good to Dorothy and supportive in all that she had done, and now she had gone and made a right royal mess of things. She sat down and dejectedly shared the morning's events. As she reached the punch line, the boys gasped in shock and chuckled at her audacity. Then her phone rang.

"Dorothy, it's Catherine Lyons. Do you have time for a coffee?" the voice said. The look on Dorothy's face sparked Trent and Scott's interest enough that they were signalling to find out who it was.

"Sure, Catherine. I'm just having some lunch at the café downstairs," replied Dorothy, surprised.

"Great, stay put, and I'll meet you down there. I need to grab a bite to eat anyway," Catherine said and then disconnected the call.

Trent and Scott were perched on the edge of their seats, wide-eyed, waiting to hear what Catherine had said.

"She's coming down here now to have some lunch with me," Dorothy said in disbelief.

The boys looked at each other with a smile, as they were keen to meet this Catherine Lyons to whom Dorothy had spoken in a way that was so out of character for her.

"You two better get out of here before she arrives," Dorothy said.

"No way. We want to meet her," said Trent.

There was no time for arguments. Dorothy saw Catherine emerge from the elevators and proudly stride toward them. Dorothy hurriedly ordered Trent and Scott to take their lunch with them and go. Catherine arrived at the table just as Trent and Scott slid out from the bench seats and excused themselves.

Sliding into one of the seats herself, Catherine asked, "Who were they? I think I recognise them."

"The tall skinny guy is Scott Crow, and the other is Trent. They are two of my best friends. You probably recognise them because they both work here at The Firm," replied Dorothy.

Catherine was reading the menu and appeared quite comfortable to be sitting opposite Dorothy despite the morning's events. Curiosity got the better of Dorothy, and she could not help but say, "So. Catherine, I guess I should apologise for what I said this morning."

The waiter arrived to take Catherine's order before she had a chance to respond. Dorothy attempted to appear collected, but she was nervously fidgeting with her hands under the table, cracking her knuckles. As the waiter walked away, Catherine said, "Honestly, Dorothy, there is no need for you to apologise. In fact, it should be me who apologises. Over the years, I have become more and more direct and impatient with my interviewees, and you just held up a mirror to me, which others have obviously been too afraid to do."

Dorothy was pleasantly relieved. This response was quite the turnaround from what she expected. She was too shocked to say anything.

Catherine continued. "On paper you seemed to have the experience and skills to do the job, but I was concerned that you may not have had the strength and tenacity to meet the challenges you would be faced with," she said. "So, in fact, it was your final comment that showed me that you actually do meet the job spec. I have recommended you for the role. In fact, I think you are a breath of fresh air, which I don't come across very often in this grey organisation."

Dorothy could bring herself to say nothing more than, "That's great."

Nothing more was required. It seemed the deal was sealed. Catherine quickly changed the topic. "So tell me about those friends of yours," she said. "Trent and Scott was it?"

One month later...

CHAPTER 7

The Merger Journey

After several more interviews with human resources and some very senior managers, Dorothy landed the role as a departmental manager. Catherine Lyons, with all her expertise in recruitment and knowledge of the business and the expectations for the role, was the perfect ally to assist her through the process.

Catherine started joining Dorothy and the boys on Friday nights for the weekly wind-downs. It was a nice change for Dorothy to have another woman around. Socially, Catherine was very different from the person Dorothy had been attacked by in the meeting room the first time they met. She was charismatic yet approachable, highly intelligent, and had an instinct for people that was unrivalled.

Over time the group learned that Catherine aspired to a career change from recruitment into organisational learning and development and that she had struggled for years to make the change become a reality. It had become a tradition now for Dorothy, Trent, Scott Crow and Tim Woods to coach and mentor each other, and it was no different with their new friend, Catherine Lyons. Together the five devised a plan, and Catherine got under way in taking the action needed to work toward her objectives.

In the following months, Dorothy took to her new role with dedication and inspiration, making dramatic improvements in her department, affecting not only productivity but representing positive impact on the bottom line. She also enrolled in postgraduate studies in an MBA program. Little did she know that her efforts and successes were being noticed and noted by the people who mattered.

Trent's career, which had rapidly risen at first, had reached a plateau, much to his frustration. In his heart, however, he knew that it was important for him to solidify his skills and knowledge, establish himself in the role, and get some more 'wins on the board' before commencing the climb again.

Scott Crow, despite his visually clumsy approach to business, was doing well. He was satisfied at this point with his career and was not looking to battle his way any further up the ladder. In recent times, he had taken a keen interest in politics. Often, in jest, he would claim that one day he might quit his job and run for a position in parliament.

Tim Woods appeared content with his job, which was located close to home, and with his ability to spend more time with his daughter. In all the time that Dorothy, Trent, and Scott had known him, Tim had not been on a date. He claimed he was not interested as he still missed his wife terribly. Although Dorothy knew it was true he missed his wife, she knew that he was surely also missing the love and affection of a partner.

After several months, it became apparent how valuable their small close-knit network had become. With Dorothy, Trent, Scott, and Catherine working in separate parts of the business, they were collecting organisational intelligence independently, which may not have meant too much on its own, but when brought together like a jigsaw puzzle revealed the big picture. Trent believed that The Firm was preparing to be acquired by another business. Tim added the final piece to the puzzle, as he had heard rumours that The Organisation that he worked for was planning to not only acquire The Firm but also to merge operations.

Based on all the lessons learned from the past, each of the friends prepared for battle in his or her own way. The one common feature to their preparation was that they all wore their best armour to work every single day to proactively place themselves in their strongest position and brace themselves for what a merger may bring. Although the economic market had improved, the employment market was still tight, and not one of them wanted to be left out in the cold as a result.

A few weeks later, and many months after Catherine's plan for a career move was in place, Catherine was approached confidentially to form a panel of specialists to work on The Firm's key talent list. She was given the responsibility to identify high potential and high performing employees in preparation for a potential acquisition and subsequent merger. This was the opportunity that Catherine had been planning and hoping for. Her recruitment experience and knowledge of the business and of many of the people within it had finally led to her working on an organisational development project. However, the opportunity was to be bittersweet, as much of what Catherine was to hear and learn was critically confidential, and she could, under no circumstance, disclose it to her closest of friends. Catherine resolved to do her utmost to protect them in any way she could in the important role she had been given.

Eventually, it became public knowledge that The Firm was to be acquired by another organisation, and the operations were going to merge. For many employees, the stress—on top of the pain that was still evident after The Firm's recent downsizing—was too much. Cynicism, resistance, and covert sabotage became apparent in pockets of the organisation. This reaction by employees simply made it easier for The Organisation to decide who to keep and who to let go. Thankfully ahead of the game,

Dorothy and Trent had prepared themselves and their teams, and developed an arsenal of artillery that would hopefully see them through the battle and help them emerge, if not victorious, at least alive.

Catherine Lyons soon learned that both Dorothy and Trent had been identified as high-potential talent and would be retained, but at this point she was not sure in what capacity. More troubling, however, was the discovery that Scott Crow's business unit was to be eliminated altogether and none of the existing staff in his area would be retained. Unable to reveal what she knew to anyone, let alone tell her close friend that he was to be dramatically affected, Catherine was morally and ethically conflicted.

One Friday afternoon, Dorothy called Catherine to confirm the night's arrangements. "Are you bringing the sushi tonight, Catherine?" asked Dorothy.

"Umm, about that," Catherine hesitated, "I'm not sure I should come tonight."

"What do you mean 'should'?" asked Dorothy, unaware of Catherine's concerns.

"I just don't think I can, Dorothy. I mean, this merger and stuff," Catherine replied as dismissively as she could.

"Is there something we should know?" replied Dorothy.

"Well, that's just it. I can't tell you guys what I know," Catherine responded.

Dorothy's hair stood on end. "Is there something we should be worried about?"

"Of course not. Well, not you or Trent anyway."

Immediately, Catherine realised she had said more than she should have, but she had only wanted to allay Dorothy's unfounded fears. In fact, Catherine knew that Dorothy was to be appointed as a regional financial manager once The Organisation had absorbed The Firm into its operations.

"Is it Scott?" Dorothy asked, her fear escalating.

"If I tell you, Dorothy, you have to assure me you won't tell anyone. Promise?" asked Catherine with a degree of trepidation.

"What is it then, Catherine?" Dorothy asked.

Catherine went on to explain the terrible situation and how Scott was surely going to lose his job.

"There has to be something we can do," exclaimed Dorothy. "We have to tell him!"

"Dorothy, you promised. You can't tell him," said Catherine. "I'll lose my job then too, and we won't have helped anyone!"

Catherine's sudden aggressiveness snapped Dorothy from her idealistic thoughts.

"But I have been thinking there might be a way to get Scott through this as unscathed as possible," Catherine said. She began to outline a possible plan.

There was a vacancy in Trent's team, and although it would be a slight demotion for Scott, the position did fit his skill set. At the very least, the job would keep him safe until the merger took place. Convincing Trent to hire him would be the easy part. The trouble would be in trying to convince Scott to change jobs, for what to him on the surface would seem an unnecessary move.

Enlisting Trent's support, in confidence, they set about concocting a story. They decided the best approach would be for Trent to explain to Scott that he was needed for the vacant role in his team to ensure the team was fully competent and positioned as a strong team heading into the merge. It was not a bad move for Trent at all, as Scott had a great deal of knowledge about The Firm that Trent did not have. They made quite a formidable team. After some coaxing, coupled with a dash of Scott's own intuition, Scott accepted the role without anyone ever noticing that intelligence had been leaked.

As the acquisition and merge took place, Trent's team was retained, with Scott on board. This was only temporary, however, until a full analysis had been done on the department's viability and contribution to the overall business. What gave the friends their greatest pleasure, however, was the surprise of Dorothy's promotion to regional financial manager.

Despite the official office relocation of The Firm still to occur, one month later, after having missed several weeks of Friday night gatherings, the group of friends - Dorothy, Trent, Scott Crow, Tim Woods, and Catherine Lyons - came together to celebrate their survival. Regardless of the good news and her friends' good spirits, Dorothy could not help but feel that things were not quite as they seemed, that something was waiting for them around the corner that they did not expect.

Three months later...

CHAPTER 8

The Treacherous Buttercups

Sitting at her new desk, in her new office, in a new building, Dorothy felt like a princess. She was perched high on her executive chair, devouring a delicious fruit salad that tasted as though the fruit had been picked fresh that morning.

Her glass-enclosed private office was flooded with natural light from the easterly view she had of the park. During the last few weeks, she had really taken notice of the fact that now when she looked out the window and saw something other than concrete structures, she could actually sense the weather as the wind blew through the trees.

Long gone was the grey Firm. The walls of the new organisation, although painted white, were decorated with bright and bold coloured artwork and furniture. The open-plan format meant she could see others at work and removed that feeling of isolation she always detested so much. Even the managers' offices were completely visible as they were surrounded by clear glass.

The artwork on the wall in her office was her favourite: a field of buttercups at sunrise, with the petals of the small yellow flowers extending to the distant horizon and the rays of the sun spraying lovingly across the field.

The members of Dorothy's new team were delightful. They were cheery, friendly, and welcoming toward her, their new manager. Although Dorothy had led project teams and worked as a supervisor and manager for many years, she found it quite a different experience to be managing an entire region. The team she was working with ensured a smooth transition for her. Consequently, Dorothy had forgotten all about her initial concerns.

Trent and Scott were still working together, and there were no signs as yet that their department would be closed down. Both said they were so busy that they could not even imagine that their contribution to the business could be seen as anything but positive and profitable.

Catherine had now successfully made the transition to an organisational development role. The experience and exposure she had gained in the acquisition and merger project ensured that she was in line for consideration when the position became available. Catherine was pleased that her friends were feeling positive about the outcome of the merger and the work environment of The Organisation. Unfortunately, however, she was unable to share in their joy. Although not appointed to work on the project directly, Catherine had heard within her department that there was some rapid change heading The Organisation's way—what exactly, she did not know. But that was not all Catherine and her friends had to worry about.

Mid-afternoon one Wednesday, Tim Woods was asked to come to head office for a meeting. His security pass did not allow him access to the floor he was visiting, so he was required to wait in the lounge area of reception on the ground floor. It was a breezy day, and as the front doors of the office automatically opened for people to enter and exit, the wind scattered leaves and litter throughout the foyer. While patiently waiting, mesmerised by the tiny tornadoes of dirt and dust, Tim could not help but overhear the receptionist talking with another woman behind the white and stainless-steel reception desk.

"Have you met that Dorothy yet, the regional financial manager?" asked the woman.

"Of course, I see her come in here every morning. But I don't often see her leave. She must work late," replied the receptionist. Tim sensed a tone in the receptionist's voice, but struggled to identify what might be behind it. The woman continued, "Yes, well, I've heard that her team thinks she is a...." Halfway through the sentence, at the critical moment, the door opened, the wind whistled, and the noise completely drowned out the two women's voices. Tim continued to watch in the hope he could lip-read what was being said, but his meeting host had suddenly appeared out of the elevator bay and was summoning Tim to follow.

As he walked past the receptionist and woman behind the desk, Tim noted their negative body language—hands on hips, rolled eyes, furrowed brows, and pursed lips. Things did not look good for Dorothy, he thought.

Tim did not have to be the one to break the bad news to Dorothy, however. The very same day, she discovered that her team's friendliness and encouragement were simply a facade.

Three weeks before, Dorothy had been asked to conduct a regional analysis and devise a quality-improvement plan to minimise waste and increase productivity. As she was so new in her role and keen to show her team that she valued their experience, she created a select project team to assist her. While she was explaining the objectives and delegating the tasks, each of the team members was enthusiastic to assist and get involved. They gave her a level of confidence she had rarely experienced before. Meeting several times during the three weeks, under Dorothy's guidance, the team had promptly pulled together an impressive improvement plan, report, and presentation.

That Wednesday, Dorothy was to deliver the report and presentation to her senior manager and the other regional finance managers from around the country, many of whom were remotely logging in for the monthly meeting. She was genuinely excited to present the body of work that she and her team had produced. As it was only her third meeting with her peers and manager, Dorothy desperately wanted to make a positive and lasting impression.

Dorothy was scheduled to deliver the final presentation of the meeting. She was well prepared. Her team had printed and bound the reports and saved the presentation to USB for her. Knowing her supportive team had done this for her, she could sit in the meeting and focus her attention to the other presentations and contribute to the group discussion.

During a break between presentations, Dorothy had an opportunity to take in her surroundings. The meeting room was inviting, with a perfectly formed boardroom-style table and comfortable chairs. One entire wall was custom-fitted wood cabinetry with secret doors and compartments disguising electrical equipment, training materials, a fridge, and catering supplies. The opposite wall was glass from top to bottom, revealing glimpses of the harbour. On the front wall was the obligatory white board, flip chart, and projector screen, while behind her was a painting. Unlike the other pieces of bright and cheery artwork Dorothy had seen around the building, this one was different. Abstract in style, the image looked like what were once rolling hills of lush grass that had now been ravaged by fire. All that was left were smouldering bushes and ash, under an angry, hot summer sky. Dorothy was brought back to the job-at-hand by the commencement of the next presentation.

When it was her turn to present, Dorothy stood and made her way to the laptop computer at the front of the room to load her presentation. She caught a glimpse of her reflection in the glass windows—a professional-looking woman dressed in a figure-hugging grey skirt suit and crisp white shirt with her hair swept neatly into a bun. This Dorothy was a stark contrast to the Dorothy that started her career as a wide-eyed graduate so many years ago, she thought.

Having loaded the presentation, Dorothy picked up the remote control and made her way to the front of the room. She tugged at her skirt, cleared her throat, and began. The title slide itself was impressively designed and offered the perfect opportunity for Dorothy to provide an executive summary of the review process and the proposed improvement plan.

The room of male peers appeared interested and alert, despite having already listened to so many other presentations. Attentive and sitting upright, they were keen to hear the rest of the presentation. Clicking the remote for the next slide, Dorothy continued her prepared speech, but noticed some puzzled looks on the faces of those around the table. Without turning around to see the screen, she could sense that what was being displayed was much brighter and lighter than what should have been a detailed colour graph. In fact, it was a blank screen.

Confused but not perturbed, Dorothy commented that there must be a problem with the technology and clicked the remote again. The slide had transitioned, but only to reveal another blank white screen. The same thing happened again and again. Dorothy's heart sank, and her mind raced to determine what could have happened and what plan of action she should take to save herself. Those attentive men were now glancing at each other with questioning looks and raised eyebrows.

Dorothy said, "Look, that's not a problem. Please each take a copy of our report, and as the presentation simply follows the same content, we can use this as our point of reference."

The participants each took a report and handed the rest to the next person around the table. Dorothy felt a sense of relief at her ability to think on her feet.

"If you could turn to page three," Dorothy said.

As she opened the report, she saw that every one of the pages behind the professionally printed title page was covered with symbols: ♌◆●♍□♋□s. There was not one legible word.

Dorothy saw a smirk on one of the faces in the room, and her manager's face revealed a combination of rage and disappointment. How could this be happening? she thought.

"Dorothy, what is this? I thought you said you were well prepared?" asked her manager.

"I was. I mean, we were. My team and I have worked extremely hard on this project and am confident in the plan I was here to present to you today," replied Dorothy, with as much strength as she could muster.

"So why is it that we are here wasting time looking at a blank screen and an illegible report?" he asked firmly.

Dorothy was going to explain how she had others in the team print the final report, copy it, and bind it, and that she had delegated the responsibility for making the final changes to the presentation and saving it to USB. She quickly realised, however, that she was the one accountable. She did not check the file on the USB after it had been given to her, and she had not opened the final printed and bound reports.

"Unfortunately, it's because I failed to check the materials before the meeting," she said. "It will not happen again." Dorothy did not know what else to say.

"No, you're right. It won't," her manager said. He pushed his chair back from the perfectly formed boardroom table and left the room. His male disciples from around the table also made their way out silently, leaving Dorothy alone, staring at the blank white screen.

Dorothy felt her lip quiver and fought back her tears. She could not understand what had happened. Was the wrong version of the presentation accidentally saved to the disk? Did the printer fail to recognise the font used in the report? It all looked fine the day before yesterday when she approved it in their team meeting. Something just did not make sense.

On exiting the lift on her floor after the meeting, Dorothy had imagined she would have been returning to her floor with positive feedback from her manager that she could share with the team. She had also imagined the team waiting eagerly to hear if their hard work and efforts had been appreciated. When she exited the elevator, however, she sensed something quite different. Many of her team members were looking at her with anticipation that Dorothy felt was not genuine. Others kept their heads down and did not smile or say 'hello' as they normally would when she walked past. Dorothy could see her assistant on the phone giggling, with her hand cupped across her mouth, unaware that Dorothy was walking toward her. While walking this 'green mile', Dorothy could feel the eyes of all the workers on the floor burning into her back. The realisation swept over her. She had been set up.

As calmly as possible, Dorothy went to her desk, checked her e-mails, collected her bag, and left for the day—at 5:00 p.m., for the first time in years.

The same day...

CHAPTER 9

The Queen Bee

Tim Woods' meeting went well—very well, in fact. Tim had recently been winning several new regional accounts and had been called into head office to meet with the national business development manager. He was not sure what the manager's motive for this meeting was, as business development was not a core function of his role, but he was pleased nonetheless that head office had taken notice of his efforts.

The national business development manager, Fiona Miller, was a tall and slender woman with a charismatic presence and the capacity to persuade and influence like no other. She had been working for The Organisation for more than six years in various capacities and was well liked by those who worked with her and for her. She was not the traditional sales type: Her focus on collaborative and genuine internal and external business relationships was the key to her success.

During their meeting, Tim and Fiona discussed his region's progress and its overall contribution to the business. They also discussed Tim's future career plans. To Tim, this seemed irrelevant as he had been captivated by Fiona's beauty from the moment they sat down. It had been such a long time since he had looked at a woman this way.

Little did he know that Fiona was equally taken with him. She had heard that Tim was a strikingly handsome man and that he was single. She even thought perhaps his appearance may have been one of the tricks to his business development success. After meeting him, however, she realised there was so much more to him. He came across in their discussion as a genuine, sensitive, and caring man. Fiona was planning to offer Tim a promotion but she could not imagine herself having to work with someone she found so attractive—especially considering the potential implications of an office romance. It was ironic really. She loved her job and the satisfaction it gave her, but she desperately wanted to meet a man and have children. She had now potentially met the perfect man, and she would have to pass on the chance of pursuing something between the two of them in order to do the right thing by The Organisation. She would just have to push her feelings aside.

"So, Tim, I would like to offer you a promotion," Fiona said, hesitating, "as a state business development manager."

Here Tim was sitting across from a woman whom he had begun daydreaming about spending cosy evenings with in front of the fire, and now she was offering him a job. The thought of seeing her every single day was a joy, but to never be able to form a personal relationship with her was too much to bear. Earlier in his career, Tim had thought that his career was the most important thing to him. But in more recent times he had been longing to share his life with a partner.

Throwing caution to the wind, he said, "Fiona, I am ever so flattered to be considered for the role, but unfortunately, I don't think that it would be the best fit for me." Tim was not sure how to continue.

Fiona interjected, "But, Tim, you would be perfect for the role."

"Of course, I think I would be great at the job, but I'm not so sure I could work in your team," he finished.

Fiona wondered what was wrong with her team—or with her. Why wouldn't Tim want to work with them?

"Why? What's wrong with them?" she asked.

"Why, nothing is wrong with them," Tim replied. "It's just, well, more that I don't think I could work with you." He blushed.

Fiona was thrilled to see that Tim was equally attracted to her. "Go on," she said, holding her breath as she waited for what Tim may say next.

"You see, I think I would rather have dinner with you," he responded.

Tim was shocked at his own forwardness, but was pleased he had found the audacity to speak up as Fiona's reply made it all worthwhile. "Your place or mine?" She grinned.

Tim did not take the job, and he and Fiona started their relationship that very evening with drinks, when Fiona met Trent, Scott Crow, and Catherine Lyons.

"Can you believe what happened to Dorothy today?" Trent asked the group.

"I know. It's horrible. If I were her, I would go to bed, pull the covers over my head, and not come out for days," Catherine said.

"When I called her to see if she were coming tonight, she just mumbled that she couldn't believe that someone could have done that to her and said she just wanted to be left alone," Scott said, with concern.

Tim shared with the group what he had seen and overheard in the reception area earlier that day. The others retold the rumour they had heard about the sabotage of her presentation, for Fiona's benefit.

Fiona was mortified. She had met Dorothy a few times and was thrilled that other women had begun to find their way up the ladder. She also knew what a boys' club The Organisation could be. Fiona had not for a moment considered that her organisation could be so pathetic as to sabotage one of its own, albeit from an acquired and merged organisation. She would have none of it.

Leading the charge, Fiona strategised with the group to devise a plan to weed out the ringleaders without their knowledge. Due to Fiona's reputation and relationships in the business, with just a few phone calls, she was able to quickly and discreetly uncover who was behind the incident.

To get the plan to work, the friends decided that Trent was the right person to visit Dorothy. First thing in the morning, he would try to convince her to return to work as though nothing had happened the previous day. He would have to come up with a plan to ensure that Dorothy arrived late, to make it appear that she was not coming in at all and lull her team into a false sense of security.

Dorothy had barely slept a wink all night. She tossed and turned as she stewed over the events of the day before. She was hurt, angry, disappointed, and miserable. How could she ever step foot back in The Organisation again? How could her team have done this to her? What did she ever do to them? Was success really worth it? Maybe she should quit while she was ahead. The thoughts continued to roll around in her head all night, like a tumble dryer full of clothes.

Just as Dorothy had seemed to drift off and capture her first moments of sleep, the sound of the alarm cut the air sharply at the usual time, 6:00 a.m. Her eyes opened wide, and she stared at the stuccoed ceiling. It was still dark outside, as it always was this time of the year, but today the dark bothered Dorothy for the first time. Why should she have to roll out of her safe and cosy bed to be confronted by those disingenuous, double-crossing monsters?

Dorothy lay flat on her back, drifting in and out of slumber, all the while reliving the disastrous meeting and the realisation that her team had planned for her to fail all along. Little did she know there was a plan in action to rectify the situation.

The group of friends rallied early to run through the plan again. As busy as bees, they fled their early morning hives and scattered to set things in motion.

Trent called Dorothy's phone multiple times, but it rang out. Clearly, she had set it on silent. No one could sleep through a phone ringing that often and for that long. He felt confident that Dorothy would still be at home, wallowing in self-pity. At 7:15 a.m. Trent pressed the buzzer at the front door of Dorothy's recently renovated Art Deco-era apartment block. There was no response. He buzzed again, for longer this time. No response. So he pressed the buzzer one more time and for a length of time so irritating that no one, not even Dorothy in her state, could resist but pick up.

A groggy Dorothy answered, "What?"

"It's me, Dorothy. Let me in," Trent enthusiastically replied.

"I would say go away, but I have a feeling you won't, so come up," said Dorothy as she pressed the buzzer and shuffled to the kitchen to put on some coffee.

As Trent entered the apartment, he realised there was going to be no trouble getting Dorothy to arrive at work late. It would simply be a miracle if he got her there at all.

Trent perched on the bar stool at the kitchen bench and waited for Dorothy to finish making her coffee and join him. She looked terrible. Her eyes were all puffy, likely from crying and lack of sleep, and she was still wearing her shirt from the day before. After a few minutes of silence,

Dorothy began to retell the events of the day before in detail, sharing the thoughts and feelings she had been tossing around in her head all night.

"I can't go back there, Trent," finished Dorothy.

Trent said nothing and waited for Dorothy to notice his silence. When she finally looked up at him, he began. "Dorothy, since when have you let a loose brick in the road trip you up and keep you down? Your career is the most important thing in the world to you," he said. "Don't let some pathetic cheating liars win this one over you. How would you be able to live with yourself if you quit now, when you have worked so hard to get here? You would be letting those people make that decision for you. Take back control."

Dorothy listened to Trent's speech and was impressed with his eloquence, which he was not known for, but his honesty was as brutal as ever. His truthful words stung. They both sat without talking, but this time no one broke the silence.

A few uncomfortable minutes later, Dorothy stood up from the bench, disappeared into her room, and closed the door behind her. At this point, Trent was worried he might have failed and that Dorothy may have gone back to bed, but to his relief, he heard the shower running. He called Fiona to let her know he would take Dorothy to breakfast and then have her at the office at 9:05 a.m. precisely.

Catherine's role in the plan was to impersonate Dorothy's personal assistant and arrange for Dorothy's manager to meet with Dorothy at 9:00 a.m. in her office to go over the material that should have been presented the day before.

Fiona's role was to enlist the support of some of her own past and present colleagues and direct her reports to secretly strategically plant themselves on Dorothy's floor just before 9:00 a.m.

Scott's job was to sit discreetly in the patisserie next door to the office to watch through the window for Trent and Dorothy's approach and then make the call to Fiona to set the plan into motion.

Just before 9:00 a.m., Fiona's decoys arrived on schedule and, as part of the plan, began to gossip with the culprits, mainly Dorothy's personal assistant and her senior business analyst. Unaware of the impending arrival of Dorothy's boss, the senior business analyst proudly boasted to all those within ear shot how he successfully made a fool of Dorothy. The analyst went on to say that since it didn't look like Dorothy was turning up today for the job only a man should rightly have, he would finally get the job he deserved.

A deep and angry voice thundered behind him. "You're right. You will get the job you deserve!"

The voice came from Dorothy's manager. He had heard every word the senior business analyst had said. It was now exactly 9:05 a.m., and as the elevator opened with Dorothy inside, her boss's voice echoed furiously across the floor. "Who else was involved?"

The plan had gone off without a hitch.

One year later...

CHAPTER 10

The Gatekeepers

After Dorothy's boss had fired the villains on her team for gross misconduct, she was able to get back to business. In fact, Dorothy's manager had been rather impressed that Dorothy had taken the blame herself and not deflected the fault of the mishap to her team. During the following months, they developed a professional relationship that ensured Dorothy was entrusted with additional responsibility and was exposed to sensitive organisational information she may not have otherwise been privy to. Her manager's coaching and mentoring meant that Dorothy was gaining invaluable experience, and unbeknownst to Dorothy, her boss had even identified her as his successor.

The following year, all Dorothy's friends were back on track with their careers, and things were running smoothly.

One evening, when the friends gathered together, Catherine Lyons was excited to share all the details of the end-of-financial-year, three-day executive conference. Catherine, now an organisational development manager and working on the conference, was thrilled with the responsibility and opportunity to have such a major impact on The Organisation.

Dorothy listened to Catherine with her undivided attention. She heard her describe the five-star hotel, the glamorous cocktail party, the expensive executive gifts, the harbour cruise at dusk, and the agenda for the daytime conference that was full to the brim of powerful and successful people.

Dorothy desperately wanted to attend the conference, but she was just a little too low on the totem pole to be invited. Not even her manager would be going. If only there was a way, she thought.

Months passed, and the financial markets were booming. The Organisation was expanding rapidly, and opportunities were ripe for the picking. Dorothy's manager was promoted to senior manager. She was thrilled for him. She believed he truly deserved it, having dedicated eighteen years of his life to The Organisation.

Still unaware of the succession plan in place, Dorothy met with her manager in his office on his last day before his move to his swish new office.

His current office was not too bad at all. It was large enough to fit not only a large desk but also a meeting table and a bookshelf full of reference titles. The view out of his office window was a combination of city skyline and harbour views. His desk was perfectly clean and orderly, with a framed photo of his wife having pride of place. Dorothy had spent countless hours in this office, working through issues and problems, brainstorming solutions, and devising strategies. She had also learned a lot and grown a lot in this role, under the wing and watchful eye of her manager.

Dorothy sat patiently in the visitor's chair as her boss replied to an e-mail. Without notice he said, "Dorothy, you have continued to impress me since we began working together. Your commitment to your career, your hard work, and your focus are commendable."

Dorothy was surprised by this outburst of favourable feedback, as he had tended in the past to coach and mentor Dorothy with constructive criticism rather than with praise.

"One of my key performance indicators was to have identified and developed a suitable successor for my role should it become available," he added. "And whether you were aware of it or not, that was you."

Dorothy was shell-shocked as she left the meeting with her manager. As she grappled with the news, she felt a combination of feelings—fear and pride, anxiousness, and excitement. Despite Dorothy's self-doubt, she was pleased with herself and knew that her path was heading in just the right direction.

Two months later, just four weeks after Dorothy had formally been appointed to her new role, Catherine Lyons called Dorothy.

"Dorothy, it's Catherine Lyons. Just to let you know, I have you on speakerphone," said Catherine.

"Sure, no problem, Catherine. To what do I owe the pleasure?" Dorothy bounced back.

Catherine was in a meeting with members of the planning committee. They were working on the final arrangements for the executive conference and collectively had come up with the idea to hold a forum session on 'Women in The Organisation'. The group had been bouncing around ideas as to which women to include on the panel, and Catherine had suggested Dorothy as an ideal candidate.

"I'm here with the executive conference planning committee, and we would like to talk to you about possibly being involved with a forum session we would like to hold," announced Catherine.

Here's her chance, thought Dorothy, to get herself to that conference. "It would be an honour, Catherine. What would the session be about?" Dorothy replied calmly.

"The title of the session would be 'Women in The Organisation'. We're considering you for the panel," explained Catherine. She then waited for what she hoped would be the ideal response from Dorothy to convince the group she would be suitable for the panel.

Dorothy did not respond immediately. Her career had required much effort to ensure her gender did not come into play, and she thought this theme was a dangerous topic. Did she really now want to expose her true thoughts on the topic to the very people she wanted to impress and keep on her side for future career opportunities?

Catherine got nervous. "Are you still there, Dorothy?"

"Yes, of course. I'm just thinking it through. It is definitely an interesting topic," replied Dorothy.

"It's not something we've covered before, and we think it would definitely spark some discussion," a man on Catherine's team responded.

Dorothy then asked, "Tell me then, what are your objectives for the forum session? How do you think The Organisation, or women for that matter, will benefit?"

Catherine Lyons watched the group, most of whom were men, glance at each other with raised eyebrows. If she did not step in now, she could see that Dorothy would miss the opportunity to share her story for the benefit of others.

"Dorothy, I think you have a powerful story to tell that would benefit not only women, but men," Catherine said, "and ultimately positively influence the culture of this organisation for the future." Catherine flicked back her mane of hair proudly.

Dorothy thought very carefully. Politically, this could be a foolish move. Could she live with herself if she was to selfishly protect her own career, at the expense of being a positive influence and making the path easier for other women to follow in the future?

Still not convinced accepting was the right move, but led by her need to do the right thing—and the chance to attend the executive conference—Dorothy said, "It does sound like a good opportunity. Who else is on the panel?"

The men in the room relaxed, and, breathing a sigh of relief, Catherine replied, "We have a few people on the list, but we need to contact them all first to gain their acceptance of the invitation before we can disclose that information."

"Of course, I understand. Please let me know if there is anything I need to do in advance of the session," Dorothy said, with increasing confidence in her decision.

"Of course," said someone else from Catherine's group. "If you are selected to form part of the panel of women, we will aim to get the discussion questions to you with plenty of advance notice to allow you to prepare your thoughts."

"Bloody gatekeepers!" Dorothy thought. Arrogating themselves the power to decide on her involvement regardless of what they led her to believe throughout the discussion.

Two weeks later, Dorothy received a cream envelope embossed with The Organisation's logo and her name written in calligraphy on the front. The envelope was impressively sealed with wax. Inside was Dorothy's invitation to the executive conference forum session. To her delight, the envelope also included an invitation to the evening harbour cruise.

Six weeks later...

CHAPTER 11

The View of Success

Dorothy arrived at the conference venue with plenty of time to spare. She had wanted to go back over her notes to ensure she clearly had in her mind the message she wanted to deliver to the audience. It was not as though Dorothy had not been in a five-star hotel before, but today this particular hotel exuded an opulence and sophistication that astounded her: the highly polished marble floors, the rich tones of mahogany wood, the heavy cream and gold drapes adorning the windows, and the beautiful ornate Victorian furniture—all just in the foyer.

The concierge directed her to the function room, where she was not scheduled to arrive for another twenty minutes.

The break-out area outside of the room was empty of people, except for a waiter who was quietly arranging teacups on a side table in preparation for afternoon tea.

The large doors leading into the room muffled the sound of the speaker's voice behind them, but they were ajar just enough for Dorothy to sneak a peek. Dorothy could not help herself. She wanted to preview the room full of people that she admired. There on the stage was the chief executive officer of The Organisation. Exuding confidence and a slight air of arrogance, he captivated the audience with his charisma and his talk of a future for The Organisation that would motivate and inspire even the greatest cynic in the room. Seated at the tables around the room were some familiar faces and other people Dorothy had not met. Of all the people in the room, only four were women. One was Sophia Williams, and. in the far corner Dorothy could not mistake the severe, polished look of Wendy West.

In all the years that had passed since Dorothy's first graduate placement, she had successfully avoided working with or for Wendy West. It was an experience she wished not to repeat. Dorothy was always disappointed that Wendy continued to survive through all the turbulent times and mergers. Her cold, direct, and impersonal management style meant that, although she was liked by few co-workers, she was valued by executive management for making the tough calls without a second thought. Catherine would often relay stories of the high turnover within Wendy West's department, which, of course, was of no surprise to Dorothy.

Dorothy was a little unnerved to know that Wendy was in the room. So unnerved that when Gabriella Monroe, the event manager, tapped Dorothy on the shoulder from behind, she jumped.

"So sorry, Dorothy. It's only me," Gabriella whispered. "Can you come with me for a moment?" Dorothy followed Gabriella away from the doors.

"I just wanted to let you know there has been a slight change of plans," Gabriella said. "The five women planned for the panel has unfortunately reduced to only three. One person has called in sick, and the other has been called back to the office."

"Oh, OK," said Dorothy. "How will this change the format of the panel discussion?"

"Not much," replied Gabriella, "but it does mean you are the most senior female on the panel. The other two are only graduates."

Before Dorothy could respond to express her concern, the two graduates ascended from the staircase. As Gabrielle moved to greet the two girls, Dorothy escaped to the bathroom to collect herself.

Looking at herself in the mirror, Dorothy said aloud, "'Not much', she says! Sure, ninety minutes of discussion between five panel participants would have meant that I was responsible for eighteen minutes, but now I'm looking down the barrel of at least thirty minutes! And the other women are just girls. How will they cope with the barrage of questions from the chauvinistic, grey-haired, executive general managers?"

Dorothy heard the outside door of the bathroom open, so she abruptly snapped quiet. The woman entering was Sophia Williams.

"Hi, Dorothy. I'm Sophia Williams," she said. "It's a pleasure to finally have the opportunity to meet you in person. I am definitely looking forward to this afternoon's forum session." Sophia shook Dorothy's hand and then gently rested her other hand on Dorothy's shoulder. "But you better get a move on. We've broken for afternoon tea, so it is time to get in there and set up."

Sophia's reassurance gave Dorothy all she needed. She proudly took centre stage, with one graduate on either side, and led an informative, contentious, and invigorating discussion among the panel participants and the audience of executive managers. With each passing question and answer, Dorothy grew more confident in her message. She could see a shift in some of the opinions and expressions of those present. If she were to do nothing more than raise awareness, Dorothy would feel as though she had accomplished something important that day. To her relief, she barely noticed Wendy West in the room.

Immediately following the forum session was one more 'closed door' session, which gave Dorothy some extra time to get ready for the formal harbour cruise that evening.

Running on adrenalin, she found herself almost skipping her way back home.

Dressed in an elegant, backless, floor-length silver dress, with her hair gathered softly at the nape of her neck, Dorothy looked stunning. The invitation had requested the presence of 'Dorothy and Partner', but as Dorothy was single she thought she would attend this one on her own. At least Catherine Lyons would be there, even though she was bringing her fiancé with her. Standing on the wharf, looking up at the grand cruise ship and watching the guests on board sipping champagne, laughing and mingling, Dorothy felt her anxiety express itself as butterflies.

Little did she know that the captain of the ship had been admiring Dorothy from the bridge. Her dress was billowing in the wind like a jib sail before it is filled with the ocean's breeze, and he could sense her hesitation. Noticing she was alone, The Captain excused himself from the bridge and made his way to the wharf to accompany the beautiful woman aboard.

Dorothy had been mesmerised by the beauty of the ship, so she did not notice The Captain appear. She was also hesitant as she was concerned at her ability to walk up the boarding plank to the ship in her long dress and stiletto heels without tripping.

"My fair maiden, may I introduce myself as the captain of this ship," said The Captain as he extended his arm to assist Dorothy on board.

Dorothy looked up at the tanned and handsome man and graciously took his strong welcoming arm. "Thank you, Captain. My name is Dorothy."

Now standing on board, surrounded by guests, The Captain took Dorothy's hand in his. "Pleased to meet you, Dorothy," he said. "I have to excuse myself to the bridge, but I do hope that you have a wonderful evening and that I might see you again." Chivalrously, he kissed her hand before disappearing into the crowd.

Catherine excitedly pounced on her. "Was that the captain? He is gorgeous! Don't look now, but everyone is looking at you."

Catherine was right. Everyone was looking at Dorothy. Were the men looking because she looked lovely tonight, or was it because they were still ruffled by her honesty in the forum session? And the women? Were they looking because she looked too lovely tonight or because their partners were looking at her?

"Put it this way," Catherine said. "You look amazing, Dorothy! Come, let's get a drink to relax." Dorothy followed Catherine to the bar.

After a drink or two, Dorothy did relax and begin to enjoy herself. She networked with those on board and enjoyed the intelligent discussion of the other guests. She now stood outside on deck at the bow of the magnificent ship with two of the male executive general managers. They had been discussing the current government's fiscal policy and were debating chances of the country electing a woman as head of state. Despite the in-depth discussion, Dorothy was still able to take in the spectacular views of the city, the glamorous homes perched on the water's edge, and the sensation of the ocean breeze on her face.

The Captain, standing in the bridge, watched Dorothy engaged in lively debate, as she elegantly tossed her hands and arms in animated gestures. He was entranced. He was also impressed that she had the undivided attention of these obviously very powerful and serious men, who were drawn by not only her beauty but also her brains. The Captain watched another woman approach the group. She had dark hair and eyes and was dressed in a black satin pants suit. She appeared to strut with an aggressiveness that he imagined was likely to be leaving high-heel indentations in the beautiful polished timber of the deck.

As the woman joined the group at the bow, he saw the group dynamic shift, and Dorothy's body language go from free and confident to restrained and self-conscious. How could a person yield that much power and influence over another simply with their presence?

As Wendy West approached the group at the bow, she interrupted Dorothy, who had been saying, "I think it's important for women to stay true to their female sensitivities even in positions of power. For instance, take Sophia Williams. She is a perfect example of a woman that has been successful while maintaining her femininity."

Catching Dorothy's remarks, Wendy responded, "Ah, yes, but like you, Dorothy, she too is here single tonight and without children to talk of."

Wendy's direct attack caught Dorothy off guard. Rather than say something she would regret, Dorothy excused herself from the group and walked inside. She could feel tears begin to emerge from a place she did not know existed. She suddenly felt trapped on this ship with nowhere to hide. Walking aimlessly, she found herself at the bottom of a narrow flight of stairs that led to a door in the ceiling above. The door at the top opened, and the man that welcomed her aboard the ship earlier in the evening was waving for her to climb the stairs and join him.

Now sitting together in the bridge, Dorothy found herself unloading her story to The Captain. She started right from the beginning of her career, explaining the journey and how important her career and success were to her, how she had kept her destination in clear view and made her way through even the most difficult of times. She also described how horrible Wendy West had been to her all those years ago, and what Wendy had just said to her outside.

The Captain looked at her with his generous and caring blue eyes and said, "Dorothy, no one should tell you what you want or what you have sacrificed. That is for you to discover and decide for yourself. If this Wendy West is all you say she is, then you need to figure out a way to get past that. On the sea," he continued, "if you spend time trying to travel around the storm but ultimately find there is no way to avoid it, you just have to face the waves head-on."

Later that year...

CHAPTER 12

The Battle with Wendy West

In her new job role as senior finance manager, Dorothy had to see and spend much more time with Wendy West. Although Wendy was more senior than Dorothy, they were often required to work together on projects and attend many of the same internal meetings. Most of the time, Dorothy successfully stayed out of her way, but at times, she felt like a slave to her resentment and fear of the woman. Dorothy had said nothing about the comment Wendy made to her that night on the harbour cruise. Dorothy's hope was that one day karma would deliver its revenge.

Tonight, however, Wendy was the last thing on Dorothy's mind. Tonight was the annual staff Christmas party, which was being held in the convention centre not far from the office. The large space enabled people like the Events Manager Gabriella Monroe, to weave their magic and create an imaginative and exciting party atmosphere. The theme was "Fairy Tales, Old and New." The centre was full of people dressed in a myriad of fairy-tale costumes. Celebrating the year were Hansel and Gretel, the three little pigs, Little Red Riding Hood, the Big Bad Wolf, Cinderella, and Snow White. More modern characters, like Ariel, Simba and Mufasa, Shrek and Fiona, and Harry Potter were also enjoying each other's company.

Dorothy and her friends had decided to dress up as the characters in *The Wizard of Oz*, as a play on Dorothy's name. Trent was Toto, Scott Crow was the Scarecrow, Tim Woods was the Tin Man, and Catherine Lyons was the Cowardly Lion. All of them were flying solo tonight: Catherine left her husband at home to look after their new baby; Tim's Fiona was away on a business trip; Scott's partner, Brian, was home sick in bed; Trent was between girlfriends; and Dorothy was still single.

The friends danced together until their feet grew tired. Then they found a bar table and huddled around it. They began to reminisce about the past. Between the few serious stories, they erupted with laughter at some of the more humorous and embarrassing ones. The camaraderie of the friends was a picture of pure friendship and support.

Wendy West watched them. How pathetic, she thought, that Dorothy and her friends would come to the party all wearing costumes in matching theme. Dorothy in her cutesy little dress, hair in braids, with her posse boosting her up, she thought. At that moment and with that thought, Wendy identified exactly how she was going to bring Dorothy down.

During the Christmas break, many of Dorothy's friends took days off from work to spend time with their families. Dorothy, however, was working through the holiday period this year, which suited her just fine. She often found it so quiet in the office that she was able to get twice her workload done in the same amount of time. With the office on skeleton staff, however, coffee breaks were lonely.

Late one afternoon, Dorothy forced herself away from her desk to make coffee in the kitchen. On the way, she passed three members of Wendy West's team. They were waiting for the elevator with wallets and bags in hand, clearly heading out to buy a real coffee. Dorothy had deliberately not socialised with these three in the past. They were thick as thieves and an integral part of Wendy's senior team, but, to be fair, none of them had done anything to Dorothy to warrant her wariness of them.

As though they were reading her mind, one of the three said to Dorothy, "Forget the coffee in the kitchen. Why not join us downstairs for a real coffee?"

Because they seemed so genuine, Dorothy gave them the benefit of the doubt. She ditched the coffee cup she was carrying and went with them downstairs for coffee.

For the next three days, Dorothy joined the three for an afternoon coffee break. Although at first Dorothy held up her guard, they all began to share stories and tell jokes, she began to relax around them. In fact, Dorothy discovered that these three did not like Wendy West either. They talked about mistakes Wendy had made and the things they had to do to cover for her. Dorothy also shared stories, mostly about her friends, the funny situations they found themselves in, and how she more often than not found herself bailing them out, but of course how often they would bail her out too. She proudly told them what a great group of friends she had and how they regularly got together, even as their lives had changed over the years. Just next week, they were having lunch together to celebrate the start of the new year.

On the fourth day, the three musketeers were nowhere to be seen at the usual coffee break time. Dorothy really did not mind, however. She wanted to get as much done as possible before the weekend began, as the majority of people would return to work on Monday.

The following Thursday, Dorothy was called into a meeting at the last minute, right before she was due to meet her friends for lunch. Thankfully, the meeting did not take long, as it turned out she really was not needed anyway, but it did make her ten minutes late. Hastily, she pushed through the door of the restaurant to see her friends, minus Tim who was still working in a regional office, listening intently to the three musketeers.

What a coincidence, she thought. She plonked herself at the table, apologised for her lateness, and picked up the menu.

"Is that what you really think of us, Dorothy?" asked Catherine Lyons.

"Think what of you, Catherine? You know I adore you guys," replied Dorothy without a second thought.

She was rushing through the menu trying to select the right meal. She usually selected a meal that never looked as good as the meal served to the person sitting next to her.

Suddenly she realised that the usual warm welcome from her friends was absent. As she looked up, she saw a smug expression on the faces of the three newcomers to the friends' table. Then she saw, sitting at the centre of the crisp white-clothed table, between the butter and the bread, a digital voice recorder.

"What's that doing there?" Dorothy asked, still unaware of the events that had unfolded before she arrived.

"After all these years, Dorothy, who would have thought you had it in you," said Scott Crow. He pushed his chair out from the table and sulked out of the restaurant.

"Had what in me?" Dorothy asked those still sitting at the table.

The three people from Wendy's team excused themselves discreetly and, with digital recorder in hand, left the friends with the chaos they had created.

"How could you say all those things about us to that bunch of monkeys?" Trent exclaimed. "And especially about me, Dorothy, after all I've done for you." He stood up and motioned to Catherine Lyons to follow him out of the restaurant.

Flabbergasted, Dorothy sat alone at the table. The reality of what had just happened began to sink in. Those three clearly were under the spell of Wendy West, and they had set her up by producing an edited version of the afternoon coffee chats she had with them the previous week. Furious and worried that Wendy had destroyed the relationships she had with the people that mattered most in her life, Dorothy remembered the kind advice of The Captain. She vowed to face Wendy head-on.

Several weeks had passed since that day in the restaurant, and no amount of phone calls, instant messages, or e-mails could convince Dorothy's friends to forgive her. To make matters worse, Dorothy had begun to feel the pressure of work and longed to share her challenges with her closest confidantes and friends. The right opportunity had not presented itself for her to confront Wendy, but Dorothy was confident it would not be long until she was able to slay the witch.

Dorothy arrived at work early one morning, when most of her co-workers were only just getting out of bed. She passed by Wendy West's office. Usually it was locked, but this morning the cleaning crew had opened the office to empty the waste bins. As chance would have it, the crew had stepped away momentarily, providing Dorothy with the perfect opportunity to sneak in and look through Wendy's drawers for the digital voice recorder. She expected the recorder to be hidden and difficult to find, but to her pleasant surprise, she found it sitting innocently in the unlocked second drawer of the desk. Briskly, Dorothy left the office and headed to her own, realising that she would need to act fast, before Wendy noticed it was missing.

Sitting in her office, Dorothy scanned through the hours of dictation Wendy had recorded until she found what she was looking for: the original recording of what Dorothy had really said about her friends. Dorothy had a management meeting that day at 11:00 a.m., and Wendy would also be attending. The meeting would provide Dorothy with her chance to bring Wendy down.

Dorothy arrived at the meeting early, as she most often did, and set herself up in the boardroom one seat to the right of the head of the table. She set up her laptop to look as though she were making last-minute changes to a document. She instead made a Web conference call to include Trent, Scott Crow, Tim Woods, and Catherine Lyons. She set her laptop microphone volume to high, muted her speaker volume, and just prayed that her friends would be at their desks at the crucial time to accept her Web conference request, so they could witness the event that was about to unfold.

Dorothy knew that Wendy was also usually early to meetings. Dorothy also knew that Wendy's motive was not to arrive early to be polite or ensure she was prepared, but rather simply to be sure to secure her position at the head of the table to assist her assert her dominance during the meeting. While sitting there waiting, Dorothy tumbled the digital voice recorder around in her hand in her jacket pocket.

As if on cue, Wendy entered the room and sat at the table next to Dorothy. Without a minute to spare, Dorothy pressed PLAY on Wendy's digital voice recorder and sat it in front of Wendy.

Without flinching, Wendy snapped, "You have stolen my property. That is grounds for dismissal."

"So, this is your recorder, is it, Wendy?" asked Dorothy.

"Of course, you know it is. You've taken that from my desk. I'll report you for that," Wendy replied.

Wendy looked at Dorothy, anticipating that she'd see a look of worry and retreat on Dorothy's face. A moment of silence fell between them, and Dorothy's voice came from the digital voice recorder loud and clear: "I could not have asked for a more supportive and caring group of friends. I love them, and I would not be the person I am today without them."

In place of a look of fear, Dorothy displayed a strength and courage she had not before felt in front of Wendy West.

"Actually, Wendy, I think I'll be keeping this recorder as evidence of your fraud in editing my words," Dorothy said. "Perhaps you should have been clever enough to delete my original words. Let's just say that from now on you will stay out of my way, or I'll have to show this to the relevant people."

Dorothy felt there was nothing more to be said. As the other meeting participants began to fill the room, Wendy seemed to look a little smaller and a little less powerful. In fact, if Dorothy did not know any better, she would have sworn Wendy was shrinking right before her eyes.

The same day...

CHAPTER 13

How the Five Were Reunited

Catherine Lyons was sitting at her desk replying to some e-mails when the Web conference request from Dorothy popped up in the bottom right-hand corner of her computer screen. Catherine had been very upset about what Dorothy had said about her and their friends. She wasn't sure she would be able to forgive her enough to go back to the way things were, so Catherine was avoiding Dorothy's calls and attempts to make contact.

Since that day, Catherine found that each of the friends grew more distant from each other and made no contact, not just with Dorothy, but with each other. Catherine realised that Dorothy really was the glue that held their friendship with each other together. She also realised how much she relied on these friends for guidance and support, which gave Catherine the courage she needed to meet the increasing demands of her job and balance those with the demands of her family life.

When she saw the Web request, Catherine tried to ignore it and continued working through her impossibly long list of e-mails. But curiosity got the better of her and she opened the request to see that the others had been invited too. Strange, Catherine thought, as it was not like Dorothy to waste company resources and time right in the middle of the working day. So she pressed 'accept'.

The video on Catherine's screen showed Dorothy sitting alone in the boardroom. Catherine said "hello" but got no response from Dorothy. She could hear Dorothy's chair squeaking as she fidgeted, swivelling her chair a bit to the right and then a bit to the left. Catherine tried again to get Dorothy's attention but received no response or acknowledgment she had even accepted the Web conference request.

She saw that none of the others had accepted the meeting request yet, so Catherine called Trent and described to him what she was watching.

Trent had just finished conducting a performance appraisal with one of his team members. He had to deliver some feedback that he knew the other person might take the wrong way. Usually he would have called Dorothy for advice before attempting a meeting like this one, and he wished he could have this time, too, as the meeting did not quite go as planned. The experience made Trent realise how much he relied on Dorothy as a counterbalance to his abrupt and honest approach with people. She softened him and often forced him to see things through other people's eyes.

Intrigued with what Catherine was describing, Trent logged into the Web conference. Trent and Catherine could hear each other speaking through the software and knew that Dorothy surely saw they had accepted her request, but she was still not responding. Trent saw Scott Crow walk past his office and called him in to ask what he thought was going on.

Just as they were about to log out, Tim Woods logged in. More importantly, Wendy West walked into view and sat down next to Dorothy. Catherine, Trent, Scott, and Tim watched intently as Dorothy's battle with Wendy West unfolded before them, and the truth was revealed.

As Dorothy and Wendy's battle came to an end and the other meeting participants began to fill the boardroom, Dorothy closed the laptop and disconnected the Web conference. Each of the friends were now left to think about how horrible they had been to ignore Dorothy and to take the word of Wendy West's three wicked monkeys over their dear friend.

At the end of the meeting, Dorothy stood proudly and assertively, picked up her laptop, and made her way back to her office. Despite the win over Wendy and the relief Dorothy felt, she was still worried. The most important thing to her was that her friends knew the truth. Still unsure if her friends had witnessed her slaying of Wendy West, Dorothy sat down in her executive chair in her office and hoped to find a missed call, an e-mail, or a text message waiting for her. To her dismay, there was nothing.

Dorothy stood up, walked to the wall of windows, and rested her forehead on the glass. She stared down at the tiny cars and tiny people going about their daily business and wondered where they were all going. Without Dorothy hearing, Trent entered the office, quietly approached the window, and rested his forehead against the glass, too.

"Where do you think they are all headed to?" asked Trent.

The two best friends slowly stood back upright. Trent noticed a small tear in the corner of Dorothy's eye.

"I'm sorry, Trent," said Dorothy.

"No, Dorothy, it's me that should be sorry," said Trent, with more emotion than Dorothy had ever witnessed him express. As Trent gave Dorothy a hug, over his shoulder she saw Scott Crow and Catherine Lyons standing at the office door, with warm and apologetic smiles on their faces.

"What about Tim?" asked Dorothy.

"Yes," Scott said, "he heard, too, and told me to tell you that we should have listened to you and trusted our friendship. That no matter what, from now on, we have to stick together."

Nothing more needed to be said.

The next day, the group of friends were reunited at lunch as they had originally planned to do weeks ago.

In the years that followed...

CHAPTER 14

Flying East Toward the Sun

Each of the friends continued on his or her path to success. Dorothy threw herself completely into her role as she felt that the success she had planned for was just within reach.

The company was advertising an opening for the group financial director role both internally and externally. Fiona Miller spotted the job advertisement on the organisational intranet and forwarded it to Dorothy. It read:

> "Reporting to the group chief financial officer, this role is a high-profile appointment with a global responsibility for The Organisation's finance function reporting to the CFO.
>
> The key responsibilities in this role include the overall strategic direction of the group and providing operational leadership to offer strategic direction, financial management, and comprehensive support to the business.
>
> The candidate will be required to manage the finance function across all jurisdictions, with general accountability for the group's performance under the guidance of the CFO.
>
> Knowledge on how to manage finance functions within a global partnership environment and experience in working within a multisite environment would be advantageous.
>
> You will be a strong financial leader who has the ability to manage and communicate with individuals of all levels and to effectively engage a large number of internal senior stakeholders."

Dorothy thought long and hard about applying for the job. She was afraid of what the consequences would be if she applied and then was not successful in being selected for the role. In the past, she had been approached directly for most of her positions. Although in those situations she still had to negotiate her way through the interview and selection process, this time would be different. She would be putting herself forward for a role that another person had not already recommended her for.

A few days after Fiona sent the e-mail link to Dorothy, Fiona called to see what Dorothy thought about the prospect of applying for the role. She thought Dorothy would be perfect as group financial director. Inside information had told her that the current chief financial officer, although extremely capable in all things strategic and financial, lacked in his ability to positively engage those around him and communicate effectively with internal and external stakeholders. He had a reputation for being quite a cranky old man at times. The CFO was in his early sixties and likely only a few years from retirement. Fiona was sure that the board was concerned that if they were to ask him to move on there may be an impact on the share price. So, it was an ideal time for Dorothy to make her move. She would be the ideal candidate to compensate for his gap in behavioural capability for the next few years, and then potentially she could be his successor. That would mean that Dorothy might not only be the first female group financial director but potentially the first female and youngest CFO in The Organisation's history.

"So what did you think, Dorothy?" asked Fiona, anticipating that Dorothy had already updated her résumé and constructed the perfect cover letter.

"I'm not sure, Fiona," Dorothy said. "It's definitely a big job that would be a challenge for me, and I would really be playing in the big boys' club."

"Are you kidding? Take a look around you, girl. We are already playing with the boys!" huffed Fiona. "This is the path you chose to take, and honestly, Dorothy, it's now or never. The timing is just right, and if you want to get to the top, there is only one way to get there. So start climbing!"

Dorothy knew Fiona had a point. Timing did have a lot to do with it. Dorothy also knew the CFO was not far from retirement age and was conscious of the fact that being successful in landing this role could mean the difference between achieving success in three to five years and achieving success in eight to ten years, while she waited for someone else to fill the role before her.

"Do you need me to tell you that I know you can do it and that I think you would be perfect for the job?" asked Fiona, with a tinge of sarcasm. "Because, Dorothy, I know you would be perfect for the job."

Dorothy did need Fiona's reassurance and felt a small boost to her confidence on hearing it. Fiona wasn't finished. "But maybe you're not ready to play in the big league if you still need the validation of others to give you the courage of your convictions." Fiona held a reflection of harsh reality in the mirror for Dorothy.

"I suppose it's just that I need to feel that people have faith in me," Dorothy said.

"Faith in the business world, Dorothy, is not an intangible hope in some unknown quantity," said Fiona. "You have to go to that board and prove to them why they should put their faith in you. You also can't expect for the rest of your career that opportunity will continue to tap you on the shoulder while you're not looking."

The two women talked it through for a few minutes more, before Fiona had to leave for the airport for a business trip, and Dorothy was left with a decision to make.

The following day, Dorothy applied for the position of group financial director. The board received her application with great interest. The recruitment and selection process was a lengthy one. Over the course of four months, Dorothy faced psychometric testing, 360-degree feedback reports, meetings with the board, and meetings with the CFO. The candidate pool had been narrowed to just two people, and Dorothy was one of them. The final stage of the process was the most gruelling of all: Dorothy would be interviewed by the people who would be reporting to her in the new role.

She was aware that the other shortlisted candidate was an external, so she thought that this final stage would be easier for her. Based on her existing relationships within The Organisation, she was in a stronger position and not coming in cold and attempting to build rapport in the allocated hour for the meeting.

As she strode toward the meeting room for the interview, Dorothy felt completely confident in the knowledge that she had made it this far in the process and that she had solid relationships with some of the people she would be meeting—that was until she saw the other candidate leaving the meeting room. He was laughing loudly with a few members of the team and was joyfully slapped on the back by another one, who had his back turned to Dorothy. As she approached, the external candidate walked past her smiling on his way out.

Dorothy suddenly felt very nervous but, without a sideways glance, walked straight toward the group of people at the door of the meeting room. The man who slapped the candidate on the shoulder turned in her direction. To her shock and horror, he was one of Wendy West's three monkeys. Dorothy's heart leapt into her throat. She knew there had been a recent internal hire into this team, but had not yet discovered who it had been. Now she knew. Frantically Dorothy ran through all the possible scenarios on how this could affect her chances, and, more importantly, how she should play her cards.

To Dorothy's surprise, the meeting went well. The team asked standard questions, all of which Dorothy was well prepared to answer. Her strategic approach was to sell herself on her transformational leadership style, her commitment to work and The Organisation, the importance she placed on teamwork, and her commitment to the development and success of those she worked with. Her responses were received positively by most people in the room. It seemed all the talk in the room was in the context of Dorothy being 'in' the job. Wendy's monkey, however, was quite obviously unimpressed—or he was fearful that Dorothy might actually get the job and become his manager.

At the end of the meeting, one of the team members told Dorothy that the team would sleep on the decision overnight. They had agreed not to discuss the candidates with each other until they met the following morning to make the final choice by way of democratic vote. Considering there were five direct reports on the team, there was no chance of a tied vote and a forced decision by the board or the CFO. Dorothy just had to cross her fingers and hope for the best, or so she thought.

The evening was hot and humid. As Dorothy walked down the stairs to the underground train station, to travel home from work, she felt the thickness of the air intensify and the heat engulf her. This sensation was almost too much to bear on top of the pressure she already felt around the impending decision.

The crowds on the platform were silent as they stood impatiently for their trains to pull into the station and whisk them away to their air-conditioned homes. Train delays and cancellations were a regular occurrence, and this night was no different. Dorothy watched as one train arrived already full to the brim with people. Only a handful of people dared to squeeze onto the carriages before the doors closed. It was clear that it would be a while before Dorothy would find herself on a train headed home. She found a bench to sit down and rest her tired feet. She wasn't in a hurry to get home, so she figured she would wait until the peak flow of people had passed so she could step onto a train in comfort, rather than being packed like a sardine into a can bursting at the seams.

As Dorothy flicked off one of her high-heel shoes to stretch her toes, she sensed that the person sitting next to her was looking at her. Clearly the world wasn't big enough, she thought. She was sitting right next to the monkey from the day's meeting.

"Oh, hi. Sorry, I didn't see you sitting there," Dorothy said, casually but cautiously. "Looks like it is going to be a long trip home tonight."

"Yeah, it does," replied the monkey.

The two sat as silently as the rest of the rail commuters. As the crowd began to thin and Dorothy had a glimmer of hope of getting on the next train, the monkey said, "I think we need to talk, Dorothy, don't you?"

Dorothy had been sitting there trying to come up with something appropriate to say. She did not want to sound as though she were trying to clear the air simply to secure his vote, so she was pleased that he raised the issue first.

"I think that's a good idea," she said. "Perhaps I should start by asking why it was that you conspired against me and did what you did under such false pretences."

The man seemed taken aback by her direct question but then softened, perhaps as he realised it was genuinely a fair question to ask of him.

"Wendy West had such a dominating power over us. In fear of our own jobs, essentially we did anything she asked of us. I know it's no excuse, but it is the reason, and I have felt terrible about it ever since," he replied humbly.

Dorothy did not immediately respond. She had mixed feelings about what he had said. She believed him when he said that he felt dominated and fearful of Wendy, because she had experienced that feeling herself. On the other hand, if he had felt so bad about it, he should have said something before now. Perhaps he was apologising only because he was concerned that Dorothy might very well become his manager.

"How do you think this could affect us working together?" Dorothy asked.

"Well, I would have to say that it could affect the possibility of us working together at all," was his response.

Dorothy considered what this remark could mean. Was it a threat?

"I overheard two of the guys on the team discussing their decision as they left the meeting room, irrespective of the agreement not to do so," he said. "They both were in agreement that they did not believe a woman could do the job."

Dorothy looked at him again in an attempt to determine if he was indeed a monkey or a man.

"So what are you saying?" asked Dorothy.

"That I think of the five people voting tomorrow, at least two of them are going to vote against you," he replied, "and potentially I am the deciding vote."

"This isn't a game, you know!" Dorothy pounced back.

"Isn't it?" he questioned.

Dorothy felt herself becoming flustered and the rumblings of her road as it potentially crumbled beneath her.

The platform was almost empty, and a train pulled into the platform. She and the man boarded and sat down opposite each other, uncomfortably.

"So what do you expect from me?" asked Dorothy, holding back the bitterness she tasted in her mouth.

"All I want from you is forgiveness, Dorothy, and for us to start again," he said.

The train emerged from the underground tunnels, and the bright orange evening sun shone brightly through the windows as the train headed east toward the coast. She slid her shoes back on, took her bag in her left hand, and stood up. She stuck out her right hand to the man and said, "Pleased to meet you. I'm Dorothy, and you are?"

The man then also stood. He took her hand in his to shake it and said, "Pleased to meet you, Dorothy. My name is Will McLean."

The votes were counted the following day, and the decision was unanimous. Dorothy was recruited as The Organisation's group financial director, reporting directly to the CFO. The role had never been held by a woman before, and Dorothy was proud that she had not only landed the role but had successfully climbed her way to senior management without compromising herself. Or so she thought.

Two years later...

CHAPTER 15

The Discovery of Success, Unmasked

Dorothy had worked long and hard throughout her career to achieve this degree of recognition. Her father had been right to tell her to stick to the path and that it would lead to success. For most people, the accomplishments Dorothy had now achieved would be considered success. Dorothy, however, could see where the path was headed, so she believed that success would only be hers once she reached the end of the road. It was the plan her father had for her all those years ago, and now she had almost reached the horizon point.

Dorothy's office had a spectacular view of the harbour, not quite the corner office the CFO had, but impressive nevertheless. Dorothy had decorated the office just how she liked it. The walls were painted in coastal ivory. There was a cream leather sofa in the corner for informal discussions, a small round glass meeting table, and four beech and stainless steel chairs. A large pot stood by the door filled with driftwood branches.

Dorothy's favourite part of her office was the original oil painting that hung behind her head while she sat at her desk. The captivating scene was of an ocean at dusk, as the sun was just disappearing behind the distant horizon line of the ocean. The sky morphed from tangerine to apricot to green to blue, with scattered soft clouds that looked like pink cotton candy. In the foreground, a small flock of seagulls flew past in formation, while in the background a lone sailboat appeared to be travelling to a faraway land. Dorothy often found herself staring into the painting and daydreaming—it carried her away to another time and place.

The past two years as group financial director had been challenging for Dorothy. Working with the cranky CFO made things more difficult than they should have been, and having to meet the needs of the board, The Organisation, and the team that worked for her increased the pressure. Dorothy was also required to work incredibly long hours to meet the needs of the global business. This coupled with regular interstate and international travel had meant that Dorothy was distanced from her father and her dear friends. She knew they all understood the incredible demands of the responsibilities she was entrusted with, but it did not ease the pain of the loneliness she often felt.

There was an impending corporate function for executive and senior management. A formal masquerade ball was to be held in the ballroom of an exclusive hotel. The invitation was made out to "Dorothy and Partner." Through the years, Dorothy had attended many corporate functions, either alone or with one of her friends or boyfriend of the time.

Last year, at her first corporate function while director, she took a boyfriend with her. They had been dating for six months, and although she thought it might have been too soon to invite him to a function like that, she did not want the other executive managers and directors to think she was a 'spinster', just as Wendy West had inferred on that harbour cruise all those years ago. The relationship with her boyfriend was already under strain as a result of the amount of time Dorothy dedicated to her job, so this event was also an opportunity to spend more time with him. The night began well, but a comment from one of the board threw the night and her relationship into a tailspin: "So, Dorothy, are there wedding bells in the future for the two of you?" he asked.

Although Dorothy knew she wanted to get married to her Prince Charming one day, she could not see how falling in love and giving herself completely to another person could fit in with her career plan. The man's innocent question (or perhaps not so innocent, she wondered) struck a raw nerve for Dorothy but also prompted a discussion she had been avoiding with her boyfriend. As her boyfriend pointed out to her later that evening, the relationship was not one of Dorothy's priorities. The demise of the relationship followed.

Dorothy was sure Scott Crow would jump at the chance to get all dressed up for the upcoming masquerade party. When she called to invite him, however, he said that he and Brian already had plans for a romantic getaway. She did not want to ask Trent again, particularly as he tended to despise fancy dress occasions. So she called Tim Woods to ask if he would escort her to the ball. Thankfully he agreed. She was even more grateful that Fiona Miller, who worked for another company now and would not be attending herself, was so understanding and was willing to lend Tim to her for the event.

Dressed for the ball, Dorothy looked at her full-length reflection in the mirrored wardrobe in her apartment. Her powder blue chiffon gown draped off her bare shoulders, cinched in at her waist, and billowed out into a full ball skirt. Her hair was formally swept up to expose her long neck and long, diamond-encrusted drop earrings. Her masquerade mask was a beautiful, angelic half-mask with antiqued crackle finish, authentic silver leaf and lace. Sparkling crystals adorned her shoes. Her look was complete, right down to her French-polished nails.

Dorothy's phone rang and startled her. The taxicab was waiting for her downstairs. After applying a quick touch-up to her lipstick, Dorothy left for the ball.

Tim lived on the opposite side of the city from the venue, so Dorothy agreed to meet him there. As the taxicab approached the hotel, she called Tim's phone to check that he was on schedule and would be waiting for her. His phone was off, so she called his home number. After it rang for so long that Dorothy was about to hang up, Fiona answered the phone in a fluster.

"Oh, Dorothy, I'm so sorry we haven't called you yet. Tim's daughter broke her arm late this afternoon at gymnastics," she said. "Tim has been at the hospital, in and out of doctor and X-ray appointments. They are preparing her for surgery as we speak. I have only come by the house to collect some things," she exclaimed.

"That's terrible, Fiona," Dorothy said. "Of course I understand. Please give my love to them both."

Sitting in the taxicab in the valet driveway of the hotel, Dorothy paid the driver and, after the bellboy opened the door for her, stepped out of the car. Two hotel staff members were holding open the wide glass doors at the entry of the hotel for her. Striding through without a second thought, Dorothy found her way up the stairs to the ballroom on the mezzanine level.

The ballroom was separated from the mezzanine-level foyer space by large mahogany doors, just like the ones she peeked through at the senior manager conference all those years ago. Although for a very different reason this time, Dorothy felt the same level of anxiety rise within her. Standing by the door were two hotel waiters dressed in masquerade, balancing trays of champagne and orange juice. After Dorothy tied her mask into place, she took a glass from one of the trays, and the waiters in unison pulled back the doors to the ballroom.

The room was decorated like a winter wonderland, with sparkling fairy lights hanging from the ceiling, crisp white tablecloths, and white and silver dinnerware. The table centrepieces were dramatic white willow branches that spilled from glass vases filled with silver-coloured stones. The men she worked with and their wives paraded the room in their glamorous masquerade attire as waiters attended to their every need.

The glittering room did not have the appeal she expected it to have. Here she was standing with her purse in one hand and a glass of champagne in the other and without anyone to share the experience with. Although she was now a director, the achievement felt empty. All these years she had thought that she had succeeded without compromising herself. Who had she been kidding? She had learned to play the game so well that she had lost all sense of herself and compromised everything to follow that path to success. "What success?" Dorothy thought. "What is success anyway? Is it this?"

The glittery room suddenly appeared to dull. The laughter among the people inside seemed contrived as it echoed and intensified to a deafening level. At that very moment, Dorothy felt the need to escape.

Dorothy left the hotel as quickly as she had arrived and found herself walking along the esplanade of the harbour. Dorothy was usually mesmerised by the harbour, but tonight she walked in a daze, completely oblivious to everything around her. After a while, she was embarrassed to realise she still had her mask on. She stopped by a pillar on a wharf to set down her purse while she untied the ribbon of the mask from the back of her head. In her haste, Dorothy had tied the bow too tightly, and it was now stuck in the curls of her swept-up hair.

From the bridge of a nearby ship, The Captain Dorothy met many years ago was, by chance, again watching her from afar. To The Captain, she was just as beautiful as she had been all those years ago. What a coincidence that she was alone again on his wharf and needing assistance.

Dorothy continued to struggle with the ribbon of the mask and finally had to start extracting the pins that held her hair up, one at a time. As she did so, she heard a vaguely familiar voice from behind her say, "Here, let me help you."

Dorothy turned around to see The Captain warmly smiling at her. With an overwhelming sense of relief, she let go of the tangle in her hair and allowed The Captain to free her from her mask.

Some time later...

CHAPTER 16

The Magic Art of Life

Squashed into a small shop-front office on the main street of an inner-city suburb, the friends were gathered together for the first time in months. There were old venetian blinds on the windows, a few melamine desks, and tired old green carpet tiles on the floor. They could clearly hear the noise from the flow of busy traffic outside. However, you could also hear the excited chatter and upbeat background music from the inside.

The group had a very special and momentous occasion to celebrate. Scott Crow resigning from his position at The Organisation. All of his friends and colleagues were here to support him.

Scott's strong beliefs in human rights and equal opportunity for all had inspired his interest in politics. For years, his friends had been encouraging him to consider running for government office. Finally Scott had decided that he was ready. He committed to his goal by quitting his job to begin his political campaign with the support of his partner, Brian. This shop-front office would be the headquarters for Scott's political campaign for election.

Watching Scott from across the office, Dorothy could see the joy and freedom he felt in the choice he had made. His feelings showed in the way he moved and interacted with others in the room. She knew he would be an ideal politician and would contribute a great deal to any community he served. She was extremely proud of him for having the conviction and belief in himself to take that leap of faith.

Catherine Lyons could see Dorothy intently watching Scott across the room and walked over to join her.

"He's brave, isn't he?" Catherine said.

Dorothy laughed. "He is, isn't he? But he always lands on his feet."

"I'm not sure I would have the courage to quit my job to follow a pipe dream," responded Catherine, in a far more serious tone than Dorothy expected considering the mood in the room.

"I wouldn't say it's a pipe dream," retorted Dorothy. "He has just discovered his true purpose and is doing something about it."

Dorothy turned to look at Catherine, who herself was now intently looking at Scott—but rather than pride, Dorothy felt Catherine's eyes reflected envy.

"What is it, Catherine? Are you OK?" prompted Dorothy.

"Yes, of course. Well, not really, I guess," Catherine struggled to say. "I am just genuinely tired of the balancing act. I feel like I give so much to The Organisation without getting anything back in return. I have been thinking lately that it might suit me to start my own consulting company so I can work the hours I want and directly benefit from the effort I put into my work."

"That sounds great, Catherine. Why don't you?" Dorothy replied enthusiastically.

With a sigh, Catherine responded, "With two kids now, a mortgage to pay, and my husband away so often, I just don't think I can."

As she considered Catherine's position, Dorothy looked over at Tim with his daughter and Fiona, giggling together as they sat around a table blowing up balloons. Tim had sacrificed his career for the love of his daughter and his love for Fiona. Through the years, Tim was the primary caregiver and supported Fiona in her career. And here they were together looking joyously happy and content with each other.

Trent was working the room. His interest in adventure sports and intrepid travelling had increased during the past few years. Not only had he become more physically fit and tanned from spending time outdoors, his sun-bleached tousled hair and more casual dress exuded an air of freedom. He had clearly decided that he was working to live now, rather than living to work. Trent was still a ladies' man, but his loyalty to himself meant that his casual relationships suited his needs and lifestyle choices perfectly.

Dorothy did not feel as though she were in a position to hand out advice to Catherine, especially considering her current state of self-doubt. Since the night of the masquerade ball, she had been questioning everything about her life—her purpose, her values, her vision for the future, and what she should do about it all. Despite how far she had journeyed in her career, she felt she was still only at the start and had a lot more to learn.

"I suspect, Catherine, that in our lives the only barriers to our success are the ones we put in place ourselves," she said. Dorothy paused and looked across at each of her friends in the room. "You just need to find the courage to believe in yourself and discover what you truly want from life. And I guess then it is just a matter of working out how to get it."

Dorothy and Catherine stood next to each other, watching the small crowd, reflecting on what Dorothy had just said and relating it to their own personal and professional lives. The party continued in full swing around them.

Three years later...

CHAPTER 17

How Dorothy Was Launched

It was a glorious morning. The sky was clear and blue, and Dorothy could hear the occasional marine navigational bell, the seagulls on their first flight of the morning, and the lapping of the calm water. The smell of salty sea air was overtaken by the delectable smell of eggs and bacon cooking.

Dorothy looked down at her perfectly manicured toes dangling over the side of the boat, high above the water. She swung her legs back and forth with a girly freedom she had not felt for a very long time. They were as tanned as they used to be when she was a child, running through the sprinkler in the backyard of her family home on hot summer days.

"Breakfast is ready," called The Captain from the galley of the boat.

Dorothy and The Captain had begun seeing each other shortly after that night, when he helped her remove her mask on the pier. He was a true gentleman. Dorothy admired his restrained sense of confidence and his ability to control a situation without effort. His calm and responsive nature made Dorothy feel nurtured and safe. She also adored how he looked at her—like she was the most beautiful woman he had ever seen.

Most of the time they had spent together was on board his own private boat. Although not quite as large as the ship on which she had first met him, this boat was impressive in its own way. The expansive flybridge deck, generous staterooms, full-width saloon, and dining area meant this boat was larger than Dorothy's own apartment. Sweeping windows spanned the saloon and dining area, enhancing the yacht's open layout with a dramatic, uninterrupted panoramic outlook. The area below deck was a combination of contemporary styling and uncompromising interior design. A blend of solid hardwood, glass mosaic tiles, and granite and marble work surfaces made the space look like a penthouse suite in a five-star hotel.

When Dorothy referred to the boat as a boat, The Captain was quick to remind her that it was a 'yacht'. Despite his reminders, Dorothy continued to get this wrong. She had always thought yachts were boats with sails.

The Captain called this yacht home. During the summer, he worked as a captain on corporate event ships. In winter, he would take his yacht to the tropics, where the weather was just perfect at that time of year, and offer private cruises to wealthy holiday makers.

Summer was coming to an end, and Dorothy knew she only had a month or so more until The Captain would be preparing to leave her. When he left last winter, she was incredibly lonely and grateful for the distraction that work offered her. On many occasions, he asked her to fly to meet him for a holiday, but Dorothy was always too busy to get away.

Her relationship with The Captain was exclusive, but still only casual, as they both knew their lifestyles did not align. Dorothy was often working when The Captain had time off, and vice versa.

Sitting across the table from The Captain, eating the breakfast he so lovingly cooked, Dorothy felt a wave of emotion. Without thinking, under her breath she said, "I love you." She gasped as she realised she had spoken her thoughts aloud. She was afraid to look up from her plate. She had promised herself not to fall in love with him because their lives were so different—she just could not see how it could work long term. Perhaps The Captain had not heard what she'd said, she thought, but she could no longer hear the clanking of cutlery on his plate and knew that he must have heard. Dorothy looked up tentatively and saw that he was smiling back at her.

"I can't tell you how happy that makes me to hear you say that," he said.

The Captain reached across the table and took her hand in his, and with the utmost sincerity and care, he said, "And I love you, too."

Dorothy had been the group financial director for several years now. Last year the CFO was scheduled to retire but, at the eleventh hour, could not bring himself to do so. Just last week, while he and Dorothy were sitting together in his office discussing the quarterly figures, the CFO told her that his wife insisted that he retire this year, so they could do some travelling and enjoy themselves before they were too old. He said he could not take the nagging any longer and that shortly he would be advising The Organisation of his retirement.

Despite her concerns about the direction of her career, Dorothy had remained swept up in the current of The Organisation and continued as though everything was fine. Everything was fine now. She was next in line to take over as The Organisation's chief financial officer. This opportunity was everything she had been working so hard for all these years. She knew that once the CFO announced his retirement, it would be three months before he would officially hang up his gloves and his replacement would step into the ring. That would allow enough time to recruit his replacement. Many people, including the CFO himself, had told Dorothy that she was the right person to take over the job.

During the regular executive general manager meeting the following week, the CFO notified his peers of his intended retirement. After some subdued cheering and clapping for him, the CEO interjected and said, "We will be aiming to recruit and announce his replacement within eight weeks. We have some very strong candidates in mind already, so the board and I don't think it will be a difficult task."

That night, Dorothy had dinner with The Captain to celebrate. Standing on the stern of the yacht, The Captain uncorked the champagne, and Dorothy held out the glasses for him to fill. They held up their champagne-filled glasses as The Captain asked, "What should we toast to?"

"To success," Dorothy rejoiced. "What else!"

The dinner of tender, barbequed, seared salmon and sweet asparagus with lemon that The Captain had cooked was heavenly. In light of her new success, everything tasted better to Dorothy. That was until The Captain said, "Dorothy, I'll be leaving next week for the winter."

The mouthful of food that Dorothy was chewing suddenly tasted dry and sour.

"Surely you don't have to. Please stay with me. You love me, don't you?" pleaded Dorothy.

It seemed to Dorothy that The Captain had been prepared for her reaction and he had scripted his response—either that or he really spoke from his heart.

"Dorothy, I do love you," he said. "But, you see, I learned a long time ago that in a relationship you must be able to stay true to yourself. If I were to stay here during the winter with you, Dorothy, for your career, I would be forgoing what has always been my dream—to run tours throughout the tropics. I feel my truest, my strongest, and my most inspired when I am at sea on my own yacht. It took me years to discover my true passion in life," replied The Captain.

Although he was delivering what should have been sad news, his eyes shone with excitement. Whenever he spoke about his adventures at sea, Dorothy was engrossed in his stories. He eloquently and passionately described every single detail and inspiring moment. She envied his passion for what he did. Dorothy had to work so tediously hard to achieve success, and it was success that inspired her. Consequently since she still had not yet achieved that success; she was still waiting to feel that same sense of passion and achievement that The Captain had for his life. She had started a journey that she was committed to seeing through. At this moment in her life however, she could now smell the sweet scent of success. The CFO job was within her reach.

The Captain continued. "Dorothy, have you found your passion? Have you recently spent the time to evaluate your life and reassess what success really is for you?" he asked. "You so often talk about this journey you are on, but, Dorothy, there is no golden path."

"You're kidding, right?" Dorothy shrieked. "I am about to reach the pinnacle of success in my career, and you are questioning me about my ability to evaluate what I want in life? What I want is to be the youngest and first female CFO ever appointed to The Organisation."

"Why?" asked The Captain.

Dorothy looked back at him with detestation. How dare he question her like that? She knew exactly where she was headed. She was focused and committed to The Organisation and the role she knew she would soon have. He should be proud of her level of achievement, not questioning it.

Dorothy thundered. "Why? Because I...." Dorothy hesitated. "Because...."

Dorothy could not answer the question. Why did she want to be the youngest and first female CFO The Organisation had ever appointed?

Dorothy was furious and scooped up her belongings to leave. As she was about to step off the yacht, she turned to

The Captain and said, "Because then I will be successful." She marched away without turning back.

Two weeks later—one month after the CFO's announcement—The Captain left for the tropics. Dorothy did not speak to him again after that night, but she had driven past the marina where his yacht was normally berthed and saw that it was gone.

The next month was packed full of discussions with the CEO and board. Corporate gossip was rampant, and Dorothy heard that they were secretly interviewing an external candidate. Regardless, all signs were positive, and she was confident that the role would be hers and there would be an announcement at the next executive general manager meeting. With the meeting now only a few days away, Dorothy was certain that she would be given an employment contract for the role in advance at any time.

On the day of the executive general manager meeting, Dorothy still had not heard anything about the new position. She had attempted to get in contact with the CEO, but his executive assistant was an exceptional gatekeeper. The current CFO insisted he knew nothing of the progress of the decision making. In fact, he had already disengaged from his role and was planning the first holiday he would be taking with his wife in years.

Dorothy was feeling incredibly nervous. She couldn't call Trent because he was off climbing some mountain. Scott Crow was busy campaigning. Tim Woods and Fiona Miller were overseas in the final stages of arranging an international adoption. Catherine Lyons' phone was redirecting straight to voice mail.

Dorothy pulled herself together and pushed her anxiety aside. Actually, she thought, it would make sense for the announcement to be made publicly in the meeting, as everyone was in support of her. In fact, Dorothy made a note to herself that she should try to look surprised when the announcement was made.

The meeting proceeded as normal. The agenda listed the new CFO appointment as the last item. Dorothy did her best to remain calm and collected throughout the meeting and to contribute as usual to the business topics being discussed. After the CEO finished the second-last item on the agenda, he leaned forward and pressed the speaker button on the conference phone which sat in front of him on the boardroom table. "Now please," he said to someone at the other end of the line.

"Surely they wouldn't be bringing in a gift or cake for the announcement, would they?" thought Dorothy. She sat upright in her chair, ready and poised.

The CEO began. "We have spent many weeks deciding on the best person for the job as The Organisation's new CFO," he said. "The person we have selected is experienced and hardworking, with exceptional financial and economic knowledge. We believe this candidate will help drive a new vision and direction for The Organisation. With unanimous board support, I am proud to announce the new CFO of The Organisation as…"

The door of the boardroom opened, and everyone turned to see what or who was coming through the door. "Please welcome Oliver Graham, your new CFO," the CEO said.

Moments later...

CHAPTER 18

Away to Sea

Dorothy sat facing the window of her office. She was uninterested in what was happening on the floor behind her. Nor was she interested in the papers on her desk, the to-do list in her diary, or the things going on outside of the window. She was disinterested in the office buildings and the cars and people hurrying through the streets. The only part of the view out of her window that interested her was the harbour. The water glistened, the moored boats swayed peacefully back and forth, the sails of the sailing boats were full of wind, and the motorboats left a trailing white wake behind them. If only she could hear the lapping of the water, the song of the seagull, and the occasional ring of the navigation bell from where she stood. Dorothy looked down at her legs, firmly crossed and hanging off her executive chair, and at her restrictive stiletto-heeled shoes. Dorothy desired that feeling of freedom that she had experienced ever so fleetingly with The Captain on his yacht.

Disillusioned and humiliated, still gazing out the window, and with her back to The Organisation, Dorothy picked up her phone and called The Captain.

The tropical winter was in full swing. The Captain had just said farewell to his first guests of the season and was preparing the yacht for the arrival of his next guests, a family of four. He was looking forward to their company. These guests had been regulars for three years, and as a result, they had become quite good friends. The children were eight and ten years old. They thoroughly enjoyed this holiday with their parents each year. Their father was an entrepreneur. Their mother, an attorney, left corporate life a few years ago to pursue her interest in holistic therapies. The couple balanced each other wonderfully and seemed to teach The Captain a different lesson every time they spent time together aboard the yacht.

While polishing the brass on the flybridge, The Captain's phone rang. He wiped his hands on the towel tucked into the back of his shorts and picked up the phone to see Dorothy's name on the screen.

He had missed her terribly. In retrospect, he realised it was inevitable that she would react the way she did when he questioned her on her life and the choices she had made. He did not regret his question, however, because he knew she was still working toward something that he was not sure was going to truly fulfil her. He wondered why she was calling now. Perhaps it was to gloat and tell him that she had become the CFO and that it was everything she had hoped it to be. In a way, he hoped that was why she was calling, as that would mean she was finally happy. On the other hand, he also hoped it might be that she missed him terribly, just as he missed her.

He picked up the phone. "Dorothy, how are you?"

"I didn't get the job," he heard Dorothy say.

"I'm so sorry, Dorothy. I know how much you wanted that job."

Silence fell between the two. The Captain could hear her sniffles and realised that she was crying. He desperately wanted to reach through the phone and take her in his arms and hold her until everything was all right again.

"What are you going to do?" asked The Captain.

Dorothy rambled about how important her career was to her and the sacrifices and compromises she had made over the years. She explained how she had told herself all this time that she hadn't been doing so, because she was so focused on following the damn 'path' and climbing the corporate ladder, and now it seemed that life had passed her by. She told him she now realised that she was not going to feel any more successful in the corner office with the title of CFO. She knew that what had motivated her was just the thrill of the challenge, not the job, not the people, and not the personal reward.

The Captain listened intently as Dorothy unloaded. Secretly, he was proud of where she found herself, that she was finally allowing herself to acknowledge and feel her truth.

Just as she finished, Dorothy said, "Is there room on that boat of yours for one more?"

The Captain chuckled to himself, but with great sincerity replied, "Of course, Dorothy, but remember it is a yacht, not a boat."

That afternoon, Dorothy typed up her resignation letter, packed up her desk, and called a taxicab. She walked to the CEO's office with a handbag on one arm and a box of her belongings on her opposite hip. As she dropped the envelope on his desk, he looked up at her in a perplexed manner. "It's not hard to guess what is contained in that envelope, especially considering you have a box in your arms," the CEO said. "Where are you going?"

Dorothy did not even pause. She strutted toward the elevators and called out over her shoulder, "I'm off in search of my success."

When Dorothy arrived home that afternoon, she packed her bags and caught a direct flight to the tropics to join The Captain on his yacht. He was so pleased to see her, and Dorothy could not have been more pleased to see him.

During the weeks that followed, Dorothy pitched in by working on the yacht but still had plenty of time for relaxation and reflection. The guests who arrived only two days after Dorothy's arrival were a wonderful family. The couple treated her like a long-lost friend and were great sounding boards and advisers. Dorothy was surprised by how admiring they were of her courage to quit her job and go in search of her true life's purpose.

She enjoyed the coming and going of all the guests on The Captain's yacht. Each of them had a different story to tell, and their successes were varied. She was intrigued but also naturally curious about their journeys and about the moments in which they knew that they had achieved success. The guests were also interested in Dorothy's story. They even asked her for advice on financial and economic matters. She was honestly surprised by how rewarding it was to share her knowledge with others.

The most liberating part of her tropics experience was the few days she spent alone with The Captain between guests' arrivals, and the staff had been dropped ashore for time off. The two of them would wake when they wanted, go where they wanted, eat what they wanted, swim when they wanted, and sleep when they wanted.

Under strict instruction of The Captain, Dorothy was not spending any time forcing decisions or fretting about what was next for her. She promised him that the only thing she was committing herself to for the time being was spending the winter with him. Her only goal was to tan her legs, hang her feet over the edge of the yacht, and dangle her toes above the crystal-clear blue waters in girly freedom.

A season later...

CHAPTER 19

Attack of the Guilts

The winter season had passed, and Dorothy and The Captain returned to the city for the summer. When they arrived at the marina, a welcoming party was waiting for them: Trent; Scott Crow and Brian; Tim Woods, with his teenage daughter, Fiona Miller, and their newly adopted daughter; and Catherine Lyons, with her husband and two children. Dorothy had fled the country as soon as she resigned from her job at The Organisation, so there had been no time for anyone to say good-bye. They were all excited to see their beloved friend for the first time since last summer.

It was almost like old times, but better, Dorothy thought. Each friend had a different story to tell, and all were eager to hear about Dorothy's decision to quit her job and head off to sea on an adventure.

Trent had just returned from a mountain-climbing expedition and told them of the life-changing experience he had while standing on a mountain top at sunset. He recalled what his guide had said to him. "Take a look over the horizon. Take a look at the sun setting over those peaks over there," the guide had told him. "Where are all the people who love and care for you in this world, and what might they be doing right at this very moment as you stand atop one of the highest peaks in the world? Be grateful for all you have, and be grateful for all those who love you and care for you, because, in a heartbeat, things can change. Remember the people you love and thank them for being there. Let them know you care about them, too, and remember that there is nothing in this world more powerful than the love and affection of the people around you. The only way to measure a person's riches is not by the material possessions he or she may have but by the relationships one maintains. Remember what is important, and focus on it." Trent was uncharacteristically emotional as he shared this life-changing moment. He finished by shocking the group with his plan to leave his job to start an adventure travel company for troubled teens.

Scott Crow animatedly detailed his successful re-election, the trials and tribulations he had faced, and the highs he had experienced. Although he knew he would have the support of the gay community for many of his initiatives, he was proud that the majority of his supporters were from the broader community. He told them about the point in time when he knew he had made the right decision to become a politician in order to make a difference. It was at a regular council meeting. A young woman with her two-year-old child was sitting in the back row, attempting to keep her child quiet and still with little success. During the question-and-answer session, she stood up and approached the microphone.

"I am a twenty-year-old single mother," she said, "and I was struggling to get a job because I was unable to complete any additional studies after finishing high school and had never had a job. But recently I attended the free job skills program started at the community centre where they taught me basic computer, customer-service, and interview skills. I just wanted to come here tonight to thank you all personally as I started working in my first job ever on Monday." The free job skills program was an initiative Scott had passed through the council despite much initial resistance from other council members. At that moment, he knew that leaving his corporate career for one of public service had all been worth it.

Tim Woods and Fiona Miller had a very different story to tell. They had an incredibly stressful but wonderful experience adopting their baby daughter from overseas. After a year of forms, financial payments, and waiting, the adoption agency sent them a videotape of a newborn baby girl. They both said the moment they saw the baby girl's eyes looking up at them on that video they knew she was their daughter. Now, five months later, they said it seemed as though she had always been a part of their lives. Fiona explained how much she loved Tim's biological daughter, but they had always wanted to conceive a child together, unfortunately infertility prevented them from doing so. Fiona always maintained hope that someday they would have a baby together. They named their wonderful healthy baby girl Amy, because it meant "beloved," just as she truly was.

Since the night they celebrated Scott's decision to enter politics, Catherine Lyons had been planning to set up her own learning and development consulting agency. Dorothy was thrilled to hear this news. After finally gaining the support of her husband, registering her business name, designing and printing her business cards, and setting up a home office, it was then only a matter of landing her first client. During the winter, after receiving a referral from a close colleague, Catherine met with a potential client and pitched her services. All the friends listening knew how difficult it would have been for Catherine to pluck up the courage for that meeting, so they were all the more excited to hear that she received the purchase order for the work just one week later. She promptly resigned from her job and began the adventure of self-employment. Catherine said she remembered her first day working from home. Her husband had dropped the kids to school. Dressed in her comfortable tracksuit and slippers, Catherine turned on the computer and began to work. She was worried that the project was only going to last a month, but she received three calls that same day from people within her network who had heard she was now consulting and were eager to meet with her to discuss her services. Catherine then knew she was finally on her way.

As Catherine finished telling her story, the friends turned to Dorothy, as though she had more of her story to tell. She had already told them about the disaster of not being offered the CFO position and her joy while sailing through the tropics with The Captain. They knew Dorothy well, however, and knew there was still one piece of the jigsaw missing. Trent asked, as if on behalf of everyone on board the yacht, "What's next for you, Dorothy?"

It was now midnight, and everyone had recently left the yacht to go home. Standing on the back deck, Dorothy looked across the water, where the reflection of the moon shone brightly back at her. Not too far off in the distance, the tall city apartments and office buildings, of which one was her own apartment and another the office building she had worked in for so many years of her life, had turned off their lights and gone to bed for the evening. Dorothy reflected on why she was unable to answer her friend Trent's question. She did not know what was next for her. She knew she needed to find her success, but she was not sure how or even exactly what it was. Perhaps she should go back to the work she knew, go back to working in one of those buildings. Maybe a break was all that she had needed. Finance was all that she knew. What else could there be?

The Captain was watching Dorothy as she stared up at the city skyline. He had wondered how she would adjust once they returned from the tropics, what she would choose to do with her life and whether or not she would get sucked back into the vortex of the familiar.

He left Dorothy with her thoughts for a while and then approached her and wrapped his strong arms around her. Her body felt tense, but then she dropped her head back onto his shoulder and relaxed against him.

"Dorothy," he said, "you can do or be anything you want to. I will support you in any choices you make."

Without thinking, Dorothy exclaimed, "But what about my plan to follow the yellow brick road? That's all I know."

The Captain wisely responded, "The plan you set for yourself when you were twenty is not necessarily the right plan for you today. Dorothy, it is important for you to reevaluate your plan based on your changing needs, wants, and values."

"But I would be failing my father," she said. "I would be letting him down." She sounded despondent.

"You know better than that, Dorothy," The Captain said. "Honestly. Not only is this life yours and not your father's, but there is only one failure and that is in falling down and not getting back up again."

He spun Dorothy around, held her face in his hands, and looked deep into her eyes. "It's time for you now to let go of your guilt and release yourself from those shackles and find your purpose, define your values, and create for yourself a vision for the future."

The following week...

CHAPTER 20

The Delicate Art of Change

It took Dorothy more than a week after her return to muster the courage to go back to her apartment. She suddenly felt so fragile and afraid. The Captain reassured her that everything would turn out fine if she just trusted herself enough to take one step at a time. To move too quickly at this stage may be counterproductive, he said.

The apartment was exactly how she had left it, just a little dustier. Dorothy was shocked by how claustrophobic she felt in the enclosed rooms and walked straight to the windows to sweep open the heavy curtains. On the coffee table sat the box that contained all the office belongings she brought home the day she resigned. She confidently picked it up and slid it onto the highest shelf of the wardrobe in the third bedroom.

Reflectively, Dorothy strolled through each room of her apartment. She noticed the contemporary Austrian crystal chandelier that hung dramatically from the centre of the ceiling in the lounge room, above the full leather sofa and chaise. The high-gloss kitchen with shiny stainless-steel appliances and her prized espresso coffee machine. The beautiful remodelled bathroom had natural-stone floor tiles, mosaic wall tiles, and a decadent spa bath. Then she entered the bedroom, which had a king-size bed, and the converted second bedroom, which served as her walk-in robe and dressing room containing her designer clothes, shoes, and bags. The third bedroom was a home office. Dorothy was surprised at her lack of attachment to most of the things that she had accumulated throughout the years.

On her way to the apartment, Dorothy had picked up the daily newspaper. It had been such a long time since she had read her hometown paper. She grabbed it from her bag, flopped onto the bed, and began aimlessly flicking through the pages.

An hour later, she woke up, not realising she had fallen asleep. She had rolled onto the paper unknowingly while sleeping. Now, as she rolled back over, one of the pages stuck to her hand. She shook her hand, but the page did not fall off. Peeling away the paper with her other hand, she noticed a job advertisement glaring back at her. The notice was small, and not set in bold type, but, for some reason, it jumped out at her from among the other text, articles, and advertisements on the page.

Before she lost her nerve, Dorothy picked up the phone and called the number of the recruitment agency. After a lengthy discussion, both the recruiter and Dorothy thought she would be more than qualified for the job.

Two weeks later, Dorothy had not only moved in with The Captain onto the yacht, she had also leased her apartment, put all her belongings into storage, and started her new job as a financial accountant for a well-respected not-for-profit organisation. The company created the position to fill a six-month paternity leave contract. Dorothy believed this job would be the perfect stopgap until she decided what it was she really wanted to do.

The office of the not-for-profit organisation was a little run-down, but it was full of life and activity. The people she worked with were passionate and earnest, with a genuine desire to make a difference in the world around them. At first, Dorothy felt like a fraud, as her motive for being there was not in line with that of the others in the office. Over time, however, inspired by the energy and enthusiasm around her, Dorothy was bouncing out of bed in the morning, genuinely excited about getting to work.

During one lunch break, Dorothy was sitting with Cynthia Greggs, the not-for-profit organisation's CEO. Cynthia was someone Dorothy admired. Cynthia took the role of national CEO four years ago and quickly brought focus and rigour to the not-for-profit organisation, which was previously a loose collection of state-based bodies. Dorothy had learned in her short time working there that, through drive, passion, and dedication, Cynthia had been responsible for ensuring the fledgling charity became unified and flourishing. She successfully developed critical partnerships with businesses and operationally refined processes and systems. Cynthia built cohesion and better communication between the state bodies and developed an important governance model. She also identified four key values for the not-for-profit organisation to focus on: support, research, awareness, and advocacy—all of which resulted in the amazing success the not-for-profit organisation had achieved in recent times.

Dorothy's curiosity won that day. She asked Cynthia, "Do you aspire to anything more than this?"

When Cynthia looked back at her in confusion, Dorothy continued, "You know, do you aspire to being a CEO of a for-profit organisation?"

Dorothy had seen the same look on Cynthia's face before, however, on the face of another whom she could not quite place quickly enough before Cynthia replied, "Dorothy, this would have to be the most rewarding job I have ever had," Cynthia said. "Sure, I might not get paid what other CEOs get paid, but in this job, I get to make a difference in others' lives and go to sleep at night with satisfaction and a clear conscience."

The Captain had noticed quite a shift in Dorothy since she began working with the not-for-profit organisation. He was quietly confident that the lessons Dorothy was learning and the change she was undertaking were going to be good for her—good for both of them. Little did he realise, however, the enormous change that lay around the corner for both of them.

The end of summer approached, and soon it would be time for The Captain to leave again. Neither of them had raised the issue as they both hoped that if they did not talk about it, they might not ever have to deal with it. One Saturday afternoon, The Captain returned to the yacht to find Dorothy lying sick in bed. She had been complaining for more than a week of feeling unwell, but she had not been sick enough to warrant spending a beautiful day in bed. That was until now.

"Dorothy, are you OK?" The Captain consoled.

"I think so," Dorothy answered, unconvincingly.

"What do you think might be wrong?" he asked.

Dorothy looked up at The Captain and saw that he was clearly terribly worried about her. She had been to the doctor earlier that week, and he had seemed quite concerned and taken blood to run a series of tests. When Dorothy had called to retrieve the results over the phone, she was asked to return to the surgery to meet with the doctor in person. This request did little to put her anxiety to rest. She returned to the doctor that Saturday morning, feeling the most ill and weak she had ever felt, to receive the results. His words were still reverberating in her head.

Dorothy sat up in bed and took The Captain's hands in hers. Her heart was beating loudly in her chest, and she wondered if she would even be able to say the words aloud. Closing her eyes, she took a deep breath, opened her eyes, and gulped. "I'm pregnant," she said.

The Captain's expression froze. She was not expecting jubilation, but she sure was hoping for some words of encouragement or support. After politely excusing himself, he left her in the stateroom all alone. She watched as he walked down the hall and up the stairs to the saloon. They had not talked about having children; in fact, they had not even talked about marriage. Dorothy was terrified that she was going to be left to do it all on her own. She imagined the worst. She was sure that The Captain was out on deck, pacing back and forth and gasping with shock.

The Captain, however, although shocked, was delighted by the news. He was, at that very moment, searching through his scuba gear for something he had hidden several weeks before and had been waiting for the right time to give to Dorothy.

Returning to the stateroom, The Captain knelt beside the bed where Dorothy was sitting. He held out in front of him a lacquered timber jewellery box. Dorothy's jaw dropped. He opened the box. A platinum solitaire diamond ring delicately sat inside, shining up at them.

"Dorothy, will you do me the honour of marrying me?"

As her tears obscured her vision, Dorothy could barely see the ring in the box held in front of her. She blinked furiously to focus and, without a second thought, responded with a resounding, "Yes."

Six weeks later...

CHAPTER 21

Catherine Lyons Becomes a King

The first trimester of Dorothy's pregnancy was not the easiest stage of her life. Dorothy worked for the not-for-profit organisation to the end of her contract, but she was relieved when it came to an end. She could then attempt to struggle her way through the torture of her morning sickness. Her doctor had promised her that the sicker she was, the healthier the baby was. Dorothy's scepticism prevented her from totally believing him, but she secretly hoped that he was right.

Knowing that Catherine Lyons had been through it all before, Dorothy often called Catherine to share her concerns and to ask for advice. Pregnancy and babies were the furthest thing from Catherine's mind, however. Since Catherine had taken the leap of faith to become a consultant and start her own business, she had been inundated with clients and exceptionally rewarding projects. So much so, she had begun looking for office space to lease so she could expand her business and hire her first employees.

After weeks of looking and not finding quite the right space, Catherine began to think her vision for her new office did not exist. She wanted to create a bright, open, and inviting space where people would want to come to work. One morning, while browsing the online property advertisements, Catherine spotted a small ad that described just what she was hoping for. Immediately she called the listed number of the commercial property agent and made an appointment to meet her there.

Catherine pulled up in her car outside of the building. It was a relatively new development, located just a fifteen-minute drive from the central business district and a two-minute walk from a train station. Catherine felt a sense of excitement, as her intuition told her that this space was the one. The office was on the ground floor, in the corner of a medium-sized building, and two of the exterior walls were floor-to-ceiling glass. Conveniently, there was plenty of parking available—another bonus. Catherine parked her car and sat impatiently waiting for the agent.

Catherine was delighted with the green space that surrounded the buildings and the café precinct just around the corner. She was desperately attempting to reduce her expectations, however, because the advertisement said that the space was already fitted out. Considering her budget for the move, that was one of the problems she had continually faced when inspecting all the other properties: Poky with lots of small boxed in offices and a lack of natural light seemed to be the trend.

Catherine must have been daydreaming. When she next looked toward the office, she saw the agent unlocking the front door. Catherine grabbed her bag and notebook and headed across the road.

As Catherine stepped inside the foyer, she fell in love with the neutral-color painted walls and laminated timber floors. She could imagine two primary-coloured contemporary lounges sitting brightly in the reception space, along with a glass coffee table neatly adorned with magazines. Around the corner would be a wonderful, open-plan office space, with enough room for as many as ten people, but with just four beech-coloured desks, strategically placed so people could focus on what they were doing. At the end of the office would be two glass-partitioned rooms: one a small meeting room and the other a manager's office. The manager's office would be small but perfectly proportioned for the glass-and-beech desk and return. The wall of the office would feature a large canvas painting of a luscious green bamboo forest. At the far left-hand corner of the office were bathrooms and a small kitchenette.

The most exciting part of the office, however, was at the left of the office just behind the entrance foyer, behind a closed door. Catherine opened the door and peeked in. The room would be perfect as a large training room, for a facilitator and fourteen training participants to engage themselves in their training. The room would be perfectly furnished with white desks, lime green chairs, inspiring artwork, and all the technology one could want in an ideal learning space.

Catherine was pleased that the agent had given her the time and space to inspect the office without interruption. As she returned to the foyer where the agent was waiting, the agent said to her, "I know it can be difficult to imagine how the space could look when you're inspecting a vacant property."

"Oh not at all," replied Catherine. "I can see exactly how this space will work perfectly!"

Four months later, Catherine was sitting at her desk in her glass-partitioned office, looking out at her wonderful and dedicated new team working away at their desks. She could hear the laughter of a group of participants emanating from behind the walls of the training room.

She unexpectedly felt hunger pains and noticed the time on her computer screen. It was almost lunchtime, and she remembered that Dorothy was due to arrive any moment. Catherine knew that it was important for her to be supportive and provide a sounding board for Dorothy, but now, with her focus on building her business, pregnancy and babies just felt so foreign to her.

167

During lunch, the women each talked about what was important to them, and each desperately wanted their old friend back. Dorothy felt that Catherine was not being as sympathetic as she might have been when she herself was pregnant or a new mother. Catherine felt that Dorothy was not giving her the business advice she might have given her before she was pregnant. They each felt as though they were on completely different trajectories.

Dorothy was perplexed by the situation and asked Catherine, "You seem to have wound up working harder and even longer hours than before. What happened to you wanting more life balance working from home?"

Catherine considered the question and contemplated her response. "I may have only a little more work-life balance, but at least now I am calling the shots. I'm probably the toughest boss I have ever had, but I'm definitely the best boss I ever had!" she said.

The friends laughed, and the mood lightened.

"I guess working from home had a certain appeal, but as soon as I realised I had something more to offer and my services were in demand, I felt the need to expand and rise to the challenge," Catherine said. "The kids are older now, and now there is time for me again. For the very first time in my career, I feel as though I have achieved something truly great, that I have arrived and discovered what all the hard work was for," Catherine added, reflectively. "Perhaps you could say I feel like I'm the king of the castle!" she said proudly. "But I suppose I could ask you a similar question. What happened to your goal of becoming a CFO, Dorothy?"

No one had directly asked Dorothy that question yet. She had been afraid to even ask it herself. The pregnancy had come at a miraculously perfect time, and it had given her the freedom and space to let go of her professional drive and simply focus on the pregnancy.

"I honestly don't know, Catherine," Dorothy replied, "but you know what? I don't think I really care at this point."

Dorothy looked around Catherine's office and said, "In fact, I don't think I want any of this. I imagine I would rather be at home with The Captain and our kids."

Catherine looked at Dorothy, amazed at her peacefulness and calm. Catherine could remember feeling the same way when she was pregnant and when her children were still babies. She wondered if perhaps women somehow were programmed this way. She also wondered if Dorothy would continue feeling the way she did now.

Two months later...

CHAPTER 22

The Land of the Twins

The doctor had advised Dorothy and The Captain to postpone their annual winter trip to the tropics, at least until the end of Dorothy's first trimester. The Captain was able to reschedule his first few bookings, which were, thankfully, all for his regular guests. Their excitement over the news that he was to become a father outweighed the inconvenience of postponing their annual holidays.

The first trimester ended, but, unfortunately, the nausea remained. Dorothy was sure she would be unable to travel at sea while feeling this sick. The Captain also realised that it was not going to be feasible for Dorothy to come with him. He was feeling torn and guilty. His clients were relying on him, and he did not want to let them down—and, of course, there was no way he would let Dorothy down either. His overwhelming desires to provide and protect were, he felt, in conflict of each other. He needed to work and fulfill his commitments to provide for Dorothy and their baby, but he also felt the need to stay with her and protect her. They had both decided to wait until the ultrasound, which was scheduled eighteen weeks into Dorothy's pregnancy, before making any final decisions.

Dorothy and The Captain waited anxiously in a small dark room for the ultrasound technician. Dorothy was lying on the bed, dressed in a surgical gown. The Captain perched on a stool, holding on tightly to Dorothy's hand. The many pregnancy books that Dorothy had purchased and read, devouring every single word, had listed copious potential concerns with the pregnancy, but had done nothing to put their minds at ease.

Both of them jumped when the ultrasound technician opened the door and entered. Clearly, each one was as nervous as the other, and they apprehensively giggled at each other.

The technician went about her business, scanning Dorothy's pregnant belly and staring at the monitor with concentration. A few minutes passed while she took photos of unintelligible shapes on the screen.

"Right, then," the woman said. "Let me now show you, and I'll tell you what I see."

Dorothy and The Captain were eager to see their baby on the screen.

"Here is the baby's head, and here you can see its arms and the beating heart," the woman said.

When she saw the baby's heart, Dorothy's own heart skipped a beat. It was simply the most amazing thing she had ever seen.

"Can we see the baby's feet?" asked The Captain excitedly.

"Well, actually no," replied the technician.

"What do you mean? Is there something wrong?" gasped Dorothy.

"Oh no, not in the sense you're thinking. There is something in the way. There is actually another baby in the way," the technician said. "You're pregnant with twins."

Neither the lapping of the water against the sides of the yacht nor the trusty sound of the marine bell did anything to assist Dorothy or The Captain in sleeping soundly the night after the ultrasound appointment. Although they were thrilled at the prospect of two healthy babies and an instant family, neither of them could quite comprehend what this would mean to their lives.

Dorothy could not imagine bringing up two babies on a boat—one maybe, but definitely not two. She could still remember The Captain once saying, "I feel my truest, my strongest, and my most inspired when I am at sea on my own yacht. It took me years to discover my true passion in life." His words haunted her, and each time she rolled over in bed to try to escape them, she heard them even louder.

The Captain, on the other hand, was tossing and turning, trying to determine the best plan of action. He knew that tomorrow he would need to cancel all of his guests for the winter season, and he would need to find a suitable home for Dorothy and the babies.

The following morning, although both Dorothy and The Captain were incredibly tired, they discussed the situation over breakfast. The Captain offered to sell his yacht, but Dorothy feared he would be filled with resentment in the future if she allowed him to do that. Dorothy suggested The Captain go away for the winter season while she move into her apartment and wait for his return. The Captain could not bring himself to leave her to manage the pregnancy on her own. If anything happened, he thought, he would never forgive himself.

After much discussion and debate, they decided that the most practical solution would be to give notice to the tenants in Dorothy's apartment, move in there together until the birth of the babies, and then take it one step at a time. The Captain would extend the period of time in which he worked for others out of the harbour, but would also offer his own yacht for private functions and events.

The plan was put into action, and everything was perfectly in place for the birth of the babies.

Despite Dorothy's fears, the birth of The Twins was uneventful—except, of course, for the moment when she held her babies for the first time. The delivery suite was painted a dusty pink and furnished with a recliner chair, a beanbag chair, and the traditional hospital bed and medical paraphernalia. In the room were Dorothy's doctor, midwife, paediatrician, and, The Captain. The Captain held one baby and the paediatrician held the other, and the two men walked toward her with the precious tiny bundles. One baby, tightly wrapped in a blanket, was placed in each of her arms. As she looked down at The Twins' perfectly formed faces, the most overwhelming sense of responsibility, protectiveness, and love overcame her. Dorothy knew it was a moment she would never forget.

The first year of motherhood was challenging. Dorothy's body had changed, and she was always tired, consumed by the needs of her newborn children. Despite this, Dorothy was in love. She loved spending time with The Twins, she loved The Captain more than ever, and she loved the family they had created together.

Her apartment definitely did not look the same. The third bedroom had been converted into The Twins' bedroom. The leather sofa was draped in blankets, the high-gloss kitchen was covered in fingerprints and the spa bath was full of toys, washers, and sponges. Dorothy would not have had it any other way. The apartment proved to be a perfectly suitable home for the four of them. It was close to the wharf where the yacht was moored and just as close to the harbour where The Captain worked on other boats. A large park was just around the corner, and all other amenities were within walking distance. In this home as time passed, The Twins had their first smiles, said their first words, and took their first steps.

Because of the kind of work The Captain did, their weekends were rarely spent together. During the traditional working week, however, they had opportunities for family time. One Monday afternoon, Dorothy and The Captain took The Twins to play in the park. Both of the children were walking now and had fiercely independent natures. Dorothy found it delightful to watch them interact with each other and entertain themselves. Next to her, The Captain sat relaxed on the park bench, with his legs stretched out in front of him, reading the newspaper. One of the twins stood at the top of a toddler-sized climbing frame, pulling on a rope. The rope was attached to a scoop-shaped bucket that had been carefully filled with wood chips by the other twin below. When the bucket reached the top of the frame, its contents emptied down a shoot and spilled out the bottom. The Twins' giggles of laughter was the sweetest sound a person could ever hear. As their giggling eased, The Twins began the process all over again.

Dorothy momentarily closed her eyes. She could hear the chatter of The Twins playing. She could sense the presence of The Captain next to her. She could feel the warmth of the sun on her face. She could smell the freshly cut grass. She believed there could be nothing more fulfilling than that.

Three years later...

CHAPTER 23

Dorothy's Wish Is Granted

On their first day of school, The Twins waved good-bye to Dorothy without a second glance and disappeared among the crowd of children pouring into the classroom.

They looked adorable dressed in their slightly oversized school uniforms with schoolbags propped onto their backs. Dorothy had chuckled to herself earlier that morning when one of the twins fell backward from the sheer weight of the backpack and was pinned to the ground like a capsized turtle. Her twin babies were no longer babies and were off to school.

During Dorothy's walk home to the apartment after dropping The Twins to school, she felt an uneasy uncertainness about the future. In recent months, she had often become frustrated with The Twins and The Captain, in most cases for no reason at all. She had also noticed The Captain was becoming uncharacteristically irritable and taking it out on her and the children.

She understood that The Captain had given up his dreams to build a family with her. Each winter season on the harbour, the demand for his services as a captain reduced significantly, and fewer customers wanted to hire him for private trips on his yacht. Dorothy thought it was likely he was becoming claustrophobic in the apartment and perhaps felt trapped.

Dorothy had put these thoughts to the back of her mind for the last few months as she struggled to see how she could meet the needs of her young children and the needs of the Captain. However, now that the children were older, she thought, it was certainly time to start thinking about the future.

When Dorothy arrived back at the apartment, there were a handful of boxes in the middle of the hallway. Attached was a sticky note from The Captain, asking her to sort through them. The Captain had been asking Dorothy to do this task for months. The boxes had been stored at the top of The Twins' wardrobe since Dorothy and The Captain moved into the apartment during her pregnancy. It was so unlike Dorothy to procrastinate over anything, but for some unknown reason, she just had just not got around to this task.

Dorothy made a cup of coffee, dragged the boxes over to the lounge room, and plonked herself on the floor. The first box was simply full of books—no wonder it was so heavy. After a quick look, she pulled out the books she had not yet read and left the rest in the box to give to charity. The second box contained what on the surface looked like sheets and towels, but Dorothy then discovered that the sheets and towels were only in the box to wrap and protect a crystal vase she had packed away when she moved onto The Captain's yacht. She put the sheets and towels in the laundry and gently placed the vase on the dining table.

When Dorothy pulled the third box closer, it rattled, which sparked her curiosity. Opening the lid, she peered inside and was taken aback by its contents. She remembered. This box was the box she had used to collect her personal belongings from her office when she had resigned from The Organisation all those years ago. Hesitantly, Dorothy reached into the box and retrieved one item at a time.

On top was her framed MBA testamur. She remembered how proud her father had been that day at the graduation ceremony. All that knowledge, she thought, and what use was it to her now? She put the certificate aside and reached into the box again.

Next she pulled out a small, slim-line, silver case. Dorothy polished the silver with her sleeve before opening the case. Inside were her business cards. She slid out one of the cards, held it up, and read her name and title aloud. A twinge of pride swept over her as she reread her title: Group Financial Director. She put the business card away and put the case to the side, on top of the framed testamur.

Reaching into the box again, Dorothy retrieved her black, dust-covered, leather-bound diary. Gently and reflectively, Dorothy wiped the cover of her diary and with her finger traced the embossed logo of The Organisation on the top right-hand corner. It felt surreal to be holding this diary again, she thought. It had been her lifeline back in the day—if it was not in her diary, it would not happen. Dorothy twirled the navy blue ribbon that dangled from the bottom of the diary around her finger. The motion felt incredibly familiar to her. Closing her eyes, she imagined herself back in her office. She could hear the drone of the air conditioning, the occasional ring of a telephone, the office chatter. She could see the bright fluorescent lights mixed with natural light streaming in through the large glass windows, bouncing off the walls and against her skin. Sitting in her executive chair, she could see the harbour views. On the wall behind her was the original oil painting of the ocean at dusk, with the sun just disappearing behind the distant horizon line of the ocean.

Without opening her eyes, Dorothy stretched her arm into the box again and placed her hand on an object that brought back very vivid and unsettling memories. She opened her eyes and violently snatched her arm back out of the box. Peering into the box, Dorothy could see the innocent-looking grey piece of technology. It was the digital voice recorder that Wendy West had used to frame her. It brought back memories that she had no interest in revisiting and less interest in ever experiencing again. Deep down, however, Dorothy felt a small sense of satisfaction in knowing that she had defeated Wendy in the end.

Dorothy left the recorder in the box when she saw the back of a photo frame that she excitedly withdrew. It was a photo of her with all her friends at The Organisation's fairy-tale-themed Christmas party.

Trent was dressed all in brown, with his hair dishevelled and a dog collar around his neck. Scott Crow was wearing his flannelette pyjamas with a rope tied around his waist, a floppy hat, and had straw sticking out of all the wrong places. Tim Woods was dressed in what looked like a silver space suit. He carried a toy axe and wore an upside-down funnel on his head. Catherine Lyons wore a cute tan suede dress, furry leg warmers, and a headband. There they all were together, having the time of their lives. Dorothy remembered the security and sense of friendship she had felt that special night.

Trent had now officially left his job and was working full-time running his adventure travel company for troubled teens. Dorothy rarely got the chance to speak to Trent these days, but whenever she did, he sounded blissfully happy and challenged every day by the work he did.

Scott Crow had become quite the politician and human rights activist. He had chosen to continue working at the local level of politics where he felt that he could have a greater direct impact on the community he chose to serve. Dorothy was continually impressed by Scott's ability to face the opposition head-on and invariably convince others to see things his way, which in Dorothy's opinion, was more often than not the right way.

Shortly after the adoption of their daughter, Amy, Tim Woods had taken paternity leave, which allowed Fiona to continue working. For them, it had been the ideal situation. Tim had missed out on his first daughter's early years and relished this second chance. Fiona was more career oriented and earned a higher salary than Tim. Recently, now that their girls were older, Tim had begun working as a financial planner and mortgage broker. Together he and Fiona had found a perfect balance for their family.

Catherine Lyons had built a hugely successful and award-winning boutique consulting business. Unfortunately, her marriage did not survive her rise to the top. Only when she was released from the guilt of her own success, was Catherine empowered to reach her greatest achievements. She was an exceptional role model for her children.

Looking back at the photo, Dorothy saw herself in the middle of the group of friends. She had her hair in braids and was wearing a blue gingham dress with red stiletto heels. Staring at her face in the photo, she wondered how another person would describe how she had 'turned out'. A failed financial accountant? Dorothy caught herself mid-thought. She had not seen herself in that light for a very long time. In fact, she had been proud to stay at home and raise her children—but now....

Dorothy wanted to run away from the thoughts that were trying to follow. In her attempt to escape, she fled the apartment and began walking aimlessly through the city streets.

Sophia Williams, a former executive of The Firm and The Organisation, had retired from full-time employment several years ago and now spent the majority of her time serving on the board of several organisations. She had just left the board meeting of The Enterprise. It was an innovative business that she found impressive in its approach to business performance, employee engagement, and leadership. The number of women in senior positions in the company also impressed her. The Enterprise, benchmarked as an employer of choice, had developed an inclusive and balanced culture. Located on the city fringe in a converted warehouse, it was

185

not only attracting the best and brightest employees but retaining them, too. Consequently, The Enterprise was growing exponentially, providing immense opportunities for those who worked there.

As Sophia stepped out of the building and onto the pavement to hail a taxicab, she was almost bowled over by a woman striding by. The woman vacantly apologised and, without looking up, helped Sophia place her falling bag back onto her shoulder.

"Dorothy, is that you?" asked Sophia.

Dorothy had been in a daze and had not noticed the woman she bumped into. Dorothy was consumed by confusion, fear, and anxiety. She felt as though she had abruptly found herself lost, without a map, and not even sure where she was headed in the first place. She did not want to have to look this beautifully dressed woman in the eye. She knew her tear-streaked face and dishevelled appearance did not accurately represent the person she was.

"Dorothy, do you remember me?" Sophia asked again.

Dorothy wiped her eyes and looked at the woman.

"Sophia?" Dorothy asked timidly. It was not that Dorothy did not recognise Sophia; she just could not believe that right now, of all times, she would randomly cross paths with the woman who had selected Dorothy for the graduate program all those years ago.

Sophia sensed Dorothy's desperation and knew better than to ask how she had been. Instead she said, "I am heading home for lunch. Would you care to join me?" Without waiting for a response, Sophia slipped her arm through Dorothy's just as a taxicab conveniently pulled up to whisk them away.

The two women of very different life stages now sat together on Sophia's back terrace overlooking the pool.

"Sophia, I have failed," Dorothy said.

"Failed at what, Dorothy?" Sophia asked curiously.

"Life, Sophia. I had a plan and things didn't turn out, so then I just let life happen," Dorothy replied, "and now I have no plan and have failed at achieving success."

Sophia looked into Dorothy's eyes with genuine care and concern. "Why not go back to the beginning and tell me the story of your journey?" she said.

So that is what Dorothy did. She told Sophia of her excitement when she was a graduate first working at The Firm, the struggle of working for Wendy West, the jubilation of landing her first permanent placement, the terror of her department closing and the potential loss of her job. She told her about her work leading the transition project team, her promotions, the battle in adapting to The Organisation's culture, Wendy's attempt to sabotage her and her eventual win, her achievement in the role of group financial director, her failure to be awarded the role of CFO, and her resignation to sail the tropics. She went on to describe working for a not-for-profit, falling in love with a free-spirited sailor, and then staying home to raise her twins.

"Oh, Dorothy, it's not sympathy you need. You need a sharp wake-up call." Sophia looked at Dorothy with a stern face but with caring eyes. "Success is not a destination. It's a journey. You have just described to me the most wonderfully successful life in which you have made a difference, overcome obstacles, and made choices. You have taken a journey that is full of success. At each of those points in time, you were successful. In fact, your greatest achievements and lessons happened when you stepped off the path and forged your own way," Sophia said.

Dorothy felt a quiet awakening inside her. "So why don't I feel successful now?" she asked. "I just wish I knew what was next and what I should do."

"Success is an individual and evolving concept, Dorothy," said Sophia. "You simply need to adjust your compass."

Sophia Williams stood up from the table they were sitting at, collected the lunch plates, and, before turning for the kitchen, said, "You didn't just meet my expectations, Dorothy. You exceeded them."

She then left Dorothy to ponder the significance of what she had said.

All the pieces began to fall into place; she understood what Sophia had said. Dorothy now knew what she was meant to do. With a sense of urgency, Dorothy thanked Sophia for her hospitability and for her words of wisdom, and departed with a sense of knowing and resolve that she had never had before.

Another three years later...

CHAPTER 24

Success Again

Dorothy stood on the timber deck of their new house, reflecting. The building was in desperate need of renovation, with its peeling paint, old carpet, and fibro exterior. On the day she and The Captain inspected the house together for the first time, they both felt as though they had arrived home. Today the nearby estuary was crystal blue, and their small sailing boat at the end of the jetty bobbed happily in the gentle waves made by passing boats. The Twins were cheerfully swimming in the pool in the backyard.

Around her and inside the house were her family, friends, and colleagues. They had all travelled to join them on their special day. She could hear them enjoying the celebration, just as she had hoped they would. After an extended engagement, looking down at her hands resting on the balustrade, Dorothy took note of the difference the wedding ring made when paired with her engagement ring. After taking a deep breath in to smell the fresh sea air, she exhaled slowly, content, self-assured, and believing in her success. In the three years since her chance meeting with Sophia Williams, Dorothy had discovered a renewed passion for her career and professional life, while genuinely maintaining perfect balance with her personal life.

The Captain had been mingling with their loved ones, and as he looked out to the deck, he saw his beautiful bride, standing alone, dressed in an antique-ivory lace-covered gown. He was transported back to earlier times, when he had watched Dorothy from the bridge of a ship. Today, however, he thought she was more beautiful, loving, and confident than ever before. He was incredibly proud of her and the life they had created together, on their own terms.

He collected two fresh glasses of champagne and quietly approached Dorothy. He gently wrapped his arms around her and offered her one of the glasses. He kissed her on the cheek and then turned her around to face their friends and family.

"I know we have already done the speeches, but there is just one more thing I would like to share with you all," The Captain declared.

The chiming of tapping on glasses echoed throughout the house, and the guests fell silent. Dorothy looked at The Captain, and a knowing smile of pride spread over her face as he said,

"May I introduce you to the new chief executive officer of The Enterprise."

Afterword

And that was the story of Dorothy's search for success. What's your success?

Just remember, follow your own path for personal and professional success.

My Journey

One of your first activities in developing a career plan is to spend time on a career review. Set aside some time to map out your job and career path since the last time you did any sort of career planning. While you should not dwell on your past, taking the time to review and reflect on the path - whether straight and narrow or one filled with many curves and dead-ends - will help you plan for the future and ultimately assist you in identifying your success.

Consider the table on the following page and complete each of the columns for your most recent job roles (you may wish to consider doing this on a separate piece of paper to give yourself more space to record your thoughts). List your current and previous meaningful job roles in ascending order and reflect on your achievements, disappointments, pivotal moments and important learnings you can take from each of those roles. This is worth doing properly, so take your time for some personal and professional reflection.

Once you have mapped your career past in the table, reflect on your course, and note why it looks the way it does. Then answer these questions for yourself:

- Are you happy with your path?
- Could you have done things better?
- What might you have done differently?
- What can you do differently in the future?

Mapping My Journey

Job role	What were my achievements/successes?	What disappointments did I encounter in this role?	What were my pivotal moments?	What were my personal/professional learnings from this role?

My Likes, Dislikes, Needs and Wants

Change is a factor of life; everybody changes, as do our likes and dislikes. Something we loved doing two years ago may now give us displeasure. So always take time to reflect on the things in your life – not just in your job – that you feel most strongly about.

Make a two-column list of your major likes and dislikes. Then use this list to examine your current job and career path. If your job and career still fall mostly in the like column, then you know you are still on the right path; however, if your job activities fall mostly in the dislike column, now is the time to begin examining new jobs and new careers.

Take the time to really think about what it is you want or need from your work, from your career. Are you looking to make a difference in the world? To be famous? Become an expert? To become financially independent? To effect change?

Finally, what are your non-negotiables? Identify your core values, beliefs, and the needs and wants that you are unwilling to compromise on and stick to them. Then also evaluate your current and potential future state against this.

Take the time to understand the motives that drive your sense of success and happiness, and use this knowledge to make choices and decisions for your future.

My Next Step on the Journey

Just as it was important to look back at your career and spend some time reflecting on your experiences, it is now vital that you look ahead. A major component of career planning and development is setting short-term (in the coming year) and long-term (beyond a year) career and job goals. Once you initiate this process, another component of career planning becomes reviewing and adjusting those goals as your career plans progress or change, and developing new goals once you accomplish your previous goals.

Consider the table on the following page and complete each of the columns as your action plan for the immediate future (you may also wish to consider doing this on a separate piece of paper to give yourself more space to record your plan). I have no doubt you have heard it before, but there's no harm in refreshing your memory....

Make your goals SMART. That is; Specific, Measurable, Achievable, Realistic, and Time bound.

So set your target and go for it!

If you need any assistance or guidance on your journey please visit www.successium.com

My Action Plan

What do I specifically want to achieve?	What action can I take to work toward that?	What resources or assistance will I need?	When will I achieve it by?

CPSIA information can be obtained
at www.ICGtesting.com
Printed in the USA
BVOW03s1444301117
501640BV00001B/5/P